the *irresistible* NOVEL

Published by Writer's Digest Books, an imprint of F+W Media, Inc., 10151 Carver Road, Suite # 200, Blue Ash, OH 45242. (800) 289-0963. First edition.

For more resources for writers, visit www.writersdigest.com.

19 18 17 16 15 5 4 3 2 1

Distributed in Canada by Fraser Direct
100 Armstrong Avenue
Georgetown, Ontario, Canada L7G 5S4
Tel: (905) 877-4411

Distributed in the U.K. and Europe by F&W Media International
Brunel House, Newton Abbot, Devon, TQ12 4PU, England
Tel: (+44) 1626-323200, Fax: (+44) 1626-323319
E-mail: postmaster@davidandcharles.co.uk

Distributed in Australia by Capricorn Link
P.O. Box 704, Windsor, NSW 2756 Australia
Tel: (02) 4577-3555

ISBN-13: 978-1-59963-825-6

Edited by **JANE FRIEDMAN AND RACHEL RANDALL**
Designed by **BETHANY RAINBOLT AND ALEXIS BROWN**
Production coordinated by **DEBBIE THOMAS**

DEDICATION

To all the writers of fiction who have been harmed by the so-called "rules" of fiction:

May you find freedom and healing, and may you sweep your readers away.

ACKNOWLEDGMENTS

Over the years of teaching at writers conferences, I had collected many of the so-called rules of writing found in Part One. But I relied on my fellow published novelists, my fellow writers conference teachers, and many aspiring novelists to amass the more than one hundred rules I ended up covering in this book. Thank you to everyone who contributed!

For Part Two, I am solely indebted to Dr. Paul J. Zak's pioneering work in the neurochemistry of reader-viewer engagement. At his website (www.pauljzak.com), you can find his various writings, including *The Moral Molecule*; he's not only a good scientist but a great communicator. Dr. Zak, may all your work lead to even more understanding of the brain—and not just so novelists can write more engaging fiction!

My editor for this book was the legendary Jane Friedman, who happened to be the publisher of Writer's Digest when I made my first proposal for the book that eventually became *Plot Versus Character*. She took a chance on me, and I'm the better for it. *The Irresistible Novel* is likewise the better for Jane's involvement. She understood and amplified what I was saying, scaled back my wacky humor, and eliminated my repetition, all with courtesy and professionalism. Thanks, Jane!

table of CONTENTS

INTRODUCTION 1

Part One:
FREE YOURSELF FROM THE PARALYZING RULES OF FICTION **15**

chapter 1: **PROLOGUES** 20
chapter 2: **DESCRIPTION** 25
chapter 3: **-*LY* ADVERBS** 31
chapter 4: **PURPLE PROSE AND PAINTED PARAGRAPHS** 36
chapter 5: **THE IMMEDIATE INCITING INCIDENT** 41
chapter 6: **"TO BE" VERBS** 47
chapter 7: **SHOW VERSUS TELL** 51
chapter 8: **BEGIN WITH ACTION** 59
chapter 9: **POINT OF VIEW** 65
chapter 10: **SPEECH ATTRIBUTIONS** 72
chapter 11: **OUTLINING** 78
chapter 12: **THAT** 83
chapter 13: **SWITCHING BETWEEN STORYLINES** 87
chapter 14: **FLOATING BODY PARTS** 91
chapter 15: **GERUNDS, PARTICIPIAL PHRASES, SENTENCE FRAGMENTS, BEGINNING WITH CONJUNCTIONS, ENDING WITH PREPOSITIONS, AND PASSIVE VOICE** 95
chapter 16: **BREAKING THE FOURTH WALL** 100
chapter 17: **WEASEL WORDS** 104
chapter 18: **READ EVERYTHING** 109
chapter 19: **ELMORE LEONARD'S RULES** 113
chapter 20: **THE BIG ENCHILADA** 119

Part Two:
THE GREAT COMMANDMENT OF FICTION 146

chapter 21: **HACKING YOUR READER'S BRAIN** 150
chapter 22: **CHARACTER BRAIN—PLOT BRAIN** 156
chapter 23: **A BRAIN CHEMISTRY STORY MAP** 162
chapter 24: **WHAT'S IT ALL ABOUT, ALFIE?** 177

Part Three:
THE BRAIN'S GREATEST HITS 180

chapter 25: **THE MONOMYTH** 182
chapter 26: **ARCHETYPES** 202
chapter 27: **ARISTOTLE'S *RHETORIC*** 216

CONCLUSION 228
ABOUT THE AUTHOR 230
INDEX 231

INTRODUCTION

What makes you love a novel?

Think of your very favorite two or three novels. Take a minute to contemplate what you love about each one. Is there anything in common between them that springs to mind? Is it that they're all character-driven stories? Are they all of a certain genre? Do they all involve a coming of age for the hero? Is the writing uniformly beautiful—sensuous prose that is a work of art in and of itself? Are they all set in a certain time or place?

For the moment, take off your critic's hat. Remove all the training you've gained as a writer or editor or critique partner, and think only about what made your heart soar and your imagination leap and your mind stretch, or whatever it was that made you love it. Do this even if the book you're thinking of was something you read, or was read to you, when you were very young. Chances are, the thing that captivated you about a story when you were younger is exactly the thing that captivates you now, or that you wish would captivate you.

If you love fiction, then something sparked that love.

For me, it was my mother singing bedtime songs to me that were not your typical lullabies. They were folk songs that told a story and always sent my mind flying. So while other kids were nodding off to "Twinkle, Twinkle, Little Star," I fell asleep with movies in my head about Tom Dooley, and the *Sloop John B,* and the defenders of the Alamo fighting ol' Santa Ana with a gleam in their eyes. I saw the doomed cowboy on the streets of Laredo, and I saw the woman coming by night to her lover's grave while wearing a long black veil.

I didn't know what those musical stories were doing to me. All I knew was that I wanted more of it. Soon I became a reader of fiction. I found novels that gave me that same rush of wonder, of transport. And years later, not only did I want more of that for myself, I wanted to do for others what had been done for me. So I became a novelist and screenwriter and artist.

For me, the pursuit of fiction is all about transport. I want to go *there* and meet that person and see that impossible sight and live that adventure. I want to be inside the adventure, feeling as if it's happening to me. And I want to give my readers the same gift.

What is it for you? What is it about your favorite novels that makes them your favorites? If you like each one for different reasons, keep zooming out. Look for one common theme that links your favorites together.

As with the other questions in *The Irresistible Novel,* it's fine if your answer is different from my answer. There's no right or wrong about why you like a novel. It simply is. But I want to help you see what you love as a *reader* of fiction. Because when you know that, you know what to do as a *writer* of fiction.

PARALYSIS OF THE RIGHT BRAIN

If you've studied the art and craft of fiction for very long, I can pretty much guarantee that you've encountered a certain frustration.

Perhaps you read a best-selling book on how to write fiction, and the author builds a compelling case for how exactly to do X—maybe description or dialogue or character creation or how to build a scene. You put the book down and apply that advice to the novel you're writing.

Fast-forward a few months, and you encounter another fiction expert. Maybe you go to a writers conference and hear someone speak on the same topic, only this person presents an equally compelling case for why you should never do X the way the other expert said you should do it.

Sound familiar? Bringing up some anxieties?

Now what are you supposed to do? You've written more than half of your manuscript according to the first teacher's advice, but now you're convinced that you shouldn't have done it that way at all. Do you finish the book the old way and then write the next book in the new way? Do you go back and rewrite the whole thing so it's in line with the new way? Do you leave it half and half?

Let's say you do the agonizing work of making it all line up with the new way. You finish your rough draft and take it to your critique group, and they all say you should've written it—you guessed it—the way you originally had.

So you tear out your hair and go back, making the full manuscript line up with how the original teacher said you should do it. You show the revised manuscript to some agents and acquisitions editors, and guess what they say? Yup: You should've written it the way the second teacher said.

With no hair left to pull out, you hire a freelance editor to tell you what to do, and she says both ways are wrong and you should really change it to this third way. Which is a way your crit group says you should never follow and is precisely the subject of an article in this month's *Writer's Digest* magazine, which espouses yet a fourth way of doing it and says that all other ways are to be avoided unless you want to get laughed at.

And that's just on one issue—our dear old X. The typical novelist has heard conflicting expert advice on more than a dozen major aspects of fiction craftsmanship. Your rough draft may please this agent in ways A, Q, and W but displease him on issues C, M, and Y—especially Y. The next agent loves the way you did Y but says you absolutely have to change W and especially A and Q.

I see this all the time. I have taught at more than fifty writers conferences, and at every one I have found dozens of novelists who were confused and frustrated by this state of affairs.

And the poor author thinks it's her problem! Now, on some level, she may suspect that writing—like painting or dancing—is highly subjective and that there are many styles that may be considered appropriate. She suspects that there might be rules that are useful for beginners that can be jettisoned by masters.

But that's not how fiction craftsmanship is presented by the experts. Based on how they present these, she comes to believe, as any rational person would, that there is a set of codified, eternal, and mutually agreed-upon laws of fiction that can be learned and mastered. She also believes, understandably, that the fiction experts teaching at conferences and writing books on craftsmanship have been inducted into this secret society, given the hidden knowledge, and authorized to give out this information to writers wanting to learn to conjure with it.

She believes, in other words, that the fiction teaching she's hearing must all be reconcilable and coherent, and if she can't figure out how to simultaneously do and not do X, it's her fault. Since everyone around her seems to know what's going on, she zips her lip, looks over her manuscript in progress, sees where she has done or not done X, Y, and Z …

And despairs.

While it would be helpful if there were a set of codified and mutually agreed-upon laws of fiction, and while some of us would like to believe that there is, there isn't. We can't imagine a scenario in, say, motorcycle repair in which you both must and must not adjust the throttle in a certain way. How could a house ever be built if the wiring must both be and not be hooked up according to someone's instructions? What if a swing set came with multiple booklets with irreconcilable assembly directions? It would be chaos.

I don't know what your experience has been with all this, but I can tell you that *chaos* would be a great word to describe the condition inside the typical aspiring novelist when he is given contradictory information from fiction teachers.

The real kicker is that the gatekeepers in the traditional publishing industry—agents and editors—have their *own* lists of must-do and must-never-do items, lists pulled together over time, which are constantly changing and don't agree with one another. For the novelist, it's not like jumping through hoops: It's like jumping through rotating hoops of flame that move and even disappear after you have committed to your leap.

The whole thing is maddening—and silly. Because what we're really talking about here are *preferences.* Preferences, and the misguided notion that there really is a right and wrong way to write fiction.

IT DEPENDS

Is there a right and wrong way to sing? Well, it depends. It depends on what effect you're trying to achieve. If you're trying to make it in the world of opera, then singing like a pop star is the wrong way to sing. If you're trying to make it as a pop star, then singing like a pop star is the *right* way to sing.

Almost no one would say that screaming into a microphone is the right way to sing, and yet Chester Bennington of Linkin Park and Danny Worsnop of Asking Alexandria and many more "screamers" make their careers in that style, and if they suddenly started singing like Pavarotti, their careers would dry up. So who's to say there's a right and wrong way to sing? It just depends on what you're trying to do.

So it is with fiction.

The so-called rules of fiction are as universally agreed-upon and universally effective as the rules of parenting. Ever had someone offer you "helpful" advice for how to parent your child that is contrary to everything you believe? And then the next person comes up, just as confident as the first, and tells you to parent your child in a way very different from what you've just heard.

The fact is that what works for one parent doesn't always work for another. And if you have more than one child, you come to the awful realization that what worked with one child may not work at all with the next one.

In *The Irresistible Novel*, I'm going to attempt to settle once and for all how you should write fiction. Not by laying out *my* preferences for how it should be done and trying to convince you to believe me, but by talking about the disputed issues one by one, showing the benefits of each side, and then asking you to decide how you want to do it.

Is it right or wrong to have a prologue in your novel? You'll hear fiction experts shout themselves blue arguing for or against. But the real answer is ... it depends. It depends on what you, the writer, prefer. No matter what you choose, lots of people are going to disagree with your choice—so you might as well do it the way you like best.

Now, there are certainly solid ways to begin a novel when you're first starting out—tried and true ways that will get your book going and will place the novel's structure in the middle of the mainstream of how most other novels start. For beginners, having guidance that will put a book in the mainstream is a great benefit. Later, when you're more sure of yourself, you may ditch those ways and go for some other way of beginning a novel, a more challenging way or a more experimental way.

Don't feel bad about wanting someone to just tell you how to write a novel. But don't fall into the trap of believing that following those instructions is the only way to write a novel.

When we're just beginning some new area of endeavor—picking up a new musical instrument, for example—we don't really want to know all the varieties of ways that it can be played. We just want to learn *one* way. "Tell me exactly how to do it. Later, when I'm feeling more confident, I might want to mess around with other approaches. But today, I have zero understanding of how to do this thing, so please just show me any good way to accomplish my goal of not sounding completely incompetent."

If that's where you are, then try some of the rules you learn about in this book or elsewhere, or follow one person's method of writing fiction, and don't think twice about it. We've all been there. But when you progress beyond the absolute beginner phase, I hope you'll no longer feel obligated to adhere to those teachings upon fear of literary death.

It's like abstract art. Any fool with a paint bucket can slosh cerulean blue onto a canvas and call it "Woman on a Sunny Day." But it's a lot more likely that an artist who has been classically trained in composition, color, balance, flow, tone, media, and technique will be able to paint "Woman on a Sunny Day" in such a way that it can be placed in a museum or sold for a million bucks.

Knowing the principles is the beginning. Adeptly using some and leaving some behind is the realm of the master. May we all reach that place.

In *The Irresistible Novel,* my first goal is to help you decide what sort of novelist you want to be. I want to free you from the paralysis of irreconcilable teachings, show you that there is no true right or wrong on these matters, and empower you to write the fiction you've dreamed of writing.

WHAT THE READER WANTS

My second goal in *The Irresistible Novel,* after freeing you from paralysis, is to teach you how to delight your reader.

What do fiction readers want from a novel? Not that special class of readers who are also novelists, but the general reader, the Walmart reader, the book club reader, the reader with scores of novels on her device, almost all of which she has read or really will read soon.

I have a high view of readers. Not that they're experts on fiction craftsmanship, but that they know what *works* in fiction. In fact, if you asked a group of fiction readers what they want from a novel, you'd hear lots of answers: to live a life different from their own. To fall in love with characters. To solve a mystery. To have their worldview reaffirmed. To be entertained. To have their thinking challenged. To feel romance again.

You probably would *not* hear any of them say, "To read a novel with the nuts and bolts of high fiction skill on display," or "To read an entire novel with no *-ly* adverbs," or "To enjoy a prologue, a satisfying three-act structure, and a book free of gerunds," or "To find a novelist who maintains a consistent point of view and keeps exposition to a minimum while making heavy use of alliteration and allegory."

You wouldn't hear them say, in other words, that the reason they love fiction is something that has anything remotely to do with fiction craftsmanship—the stuff we all have so much angst about.

Let's talk for a minute about the difference between storytelling and fiction craftsmanship. Fiction craftsmanship consists of the things *Writer's Digest* publishes books about: great characters, good dialogue, show versus tell, point of view (POV), three-act structure, description, how to begin a novel, etc. It also includes things like passive voice, "to be" verbs, speech attributions (like *said* or *queried*), gerunds, run-on sentences, and beats.

Storytelling, on the other hand, mainly refers to how compelling and engaging a novel is. It's that ineffable thing that makes a reader lose track of time and become carried away by a novel. The *transport* I delighted in as a child. It's the style and sequence of conveying the events of the book that comprise the narrative event as a whole.

Fiction craftsmanship is the nuts and bolts of how to write a novel. Great storytelling is the magic that may or may not arise in a novel and that may or may not have anything to do with craftsmanship.

In my opinion, the end reader wouldn't know good fiction craftsmanship if it bit her on the nose. Don't get me wrong: I'm not saying that typical readers don't know good fiction. I'm saying they don't know what goes on under the hood. The brass tacks of "to be" verbs or speech attributions or beats or description are invisible to them—as they should be. It's those of us in the publishing industry who get so worked up about such things, but if the intended audience doesn't know or care, it raises a few questions.

Now, I'm not saying we should pursue bad fiction craftsmanship. I actually do think that strong fiction craft causes a novel to be better than it would've been. What I'm saying is that fiction craftsmanship, high or low, is not the primary thing that causes a reader to stick with a novel or put it down.

I've heard the argument that readers may not be able to articulate why they don't like a novel, but what they're really sensing is low fiction craftsmanship. I disagree. As I said, I think high fiction skills will help a novel and low fiction skills will hurt a novel. But I've seen too many best-selling novels with absolutely atrocious fiction craftsmanship to make me believe that the majority of readers will "sense" low fiction skill and put a book down because of that.

What makes a reader put a novel down isn't that she spots one too many POV errors but that she gets bored. It's not that the fiction craftsmanship is too low quality but that the storytelling failed her.

Frankly, the typical novel reader doesn't care about fiction craftsmanship in the least. This is why so many terribly written novels become blockbusters and why so many "correctly" written novels find themselves on the clearance bin. The fiction skills of the author are simply not the issue. Readers have more sense than that.

It's not that bad craftsmanship sells and good craftsmanship doesn't, or vice versa. It's that the entire issue is moot. For the general reader of fiction, what makes her love a novel is not that the dialogue is free of speech attributions but that *the book simply captures her.* She may not be able to articulate what it was that made her unable to put the book down, but it engaged her. It hooked her, and then it kept her hooked until the end. That's great storytelling. How the book accomplished that magic doesn't matter to her. What matters is that it did. So she will tell everyone she knows about this amazing book, and she'll buy everything else this author has written.

What a reader wants from fiction is to be swept away. Enchanted. Transported. Mesmerized. Enthralled. Engaged. Grabbed by the collar. Hooked and reeled in.

You can do every single fiction craftsmanship thing "wrong" and still captivate your reader. And you can do every craftsmanship thing "right" and still *not* captivate your reader.

In the end, the fiction craftsmanship didn't matter at all.

That hurts to say, given that I'm a fiction teacher. I do believe that certain matters of fiction craftsmanship can enhance or reduce a reader's engagement with a novel, as I've said, but I can also find hundreds of novels that break even those rules and yet nevertheless become bestsellers.

I'm going to give one, and only one, rule of fiction in this book. At the risk of sounding all authoritative and thereby undoing what I've been saying so far, I'll even call it a commandment. But I think you'll like it.

The great commandment of fiction is this: *You must engage your reader from beginning to end.*

Do that, and don't stress about the rest. The reader will thank you.

WHAT ABOUT THE GATEKEEPERS?

It's all very nice for me to tell you to just write the way you want and forget about everything else. But what about the agents and editors and their rotating hoops of flame?

If I were writing this book in 2005, I wouldn't have been able to tell you to disregard the rules. Back then, and for generations before, traditional publishing was the only game in town for "real" authors (such was the perception, anyway). But now a revolution has happened and is still happening. Now, "real" authors are skipping the traditional publishing route altogether and going directly to readers through e-publishing, print-on-demand, and similar options.

So it is entirely possible for you to give no regard whatsoever to the agents and editors and others in traditional publishing. I'm not saying it's wise to do so—just that it's possible. In that case, by all means write the book exactly the way you want to and don't have a second thought about doing so.

Many authors, however, ascribe to the proverb "It is more blessed to be paid than to pay," and I concur. Traditional publishing will (usually) pay the author an advance, while publishing the book yourself will likely require an investment in cover design, editing, e-book conversion, ISBNs, etc. Novelists who want to go the traditional route still need to sort through the shifting and irreconcilable beliefs of agents and editors about what constitutes good fiction craft.

If that's you, I still want you to learn what you prefer as a novelist, and I still want you to be free of the paralysis caused by the disagreement between fiction teachers. But you'll have to do it under the extra layer of complexity of trying to guess whether the agent or editor is going to hate or love prologues, description, first-person present tense, and everything else.

Here's how I recommend you do it.

First, do your research. Some agents (and a few editors) want you to know their preferences regarding these things. Check their blogs and official websites. Ask them directly, if you can find an e-mail address or phone number. If you can find out right now that the person dislikes prologues, and you've got one, maybe you can save yourself some grief by not submitting it to that person.

Second, you still have to decide where you're going to come down on all the issues debated by fiction teachers. You're either going to have a prologue or you're not going to have one. You're either going to try to avoid gerunds for the most part or you're not. You're either going to stick with *said* and *asked* as speech attributions most of the time or you're going to add *opined*, *queried*, and *eulogized*. Read this book and decide where you fall on each of these issues. Then send the book out to the agents and editors in question.

Third, know that you're not going to please everyone. You should expect to receive lots of rejection letters. If you get any sort of explanation about why your book was rejected, it may very well be about craft issues. And if you get multiple rejections that cite craft issues, it's likely that those comments will disagree with one another. (If several responders agree on what you should work on, it's worth taking a hard look at that issue. But it's still not necessarily something you should change.) If you're expecting this sort of response to your writing, it will be less likely to drive you to drink.

Fourth, be ready to make a hard choice. Early in my career, I submitted a medieval novel to a traditional publisher. One editor really liked the book but didn't like that I'd set it in first-person present tense. He asked if I'd be willing to change it to a more traditional third-person past tense. If I was willing to do so, he'd consider publishing the book.

Suddenly I had a difficult choice to make. Did I want to do the work to change the tense and person as the publisher requested, or was I going to stick to my guns and look for a different publisher? At this point, that was the only publisher even halfway interested in the book. So I decided to revise the sample chapters

Now, I could've kept it the same and been justified in doing so. On other projects, I have decided *not* to do what the publisher requested, even knowing that such a choice would shut that door in my face.

What's the end of the story? I submitted the revised proposal to the editor and ... they still didn't publish it. Gah! But I was glad I'd made the effort. I was also glad I hadn't thrown out the original version.

Eventually, you have to choose Door One and shut Door Two if you ever want to get the manuscript completed. And when you send it out to agents and editors, it's simply inevitable that you'll set off one or more of their never-do-this triggers. Accept it.

A WORD ABOUT CRITIQUE GROUPS

I believe in the power of writing peers to help elevate your fiction. Critique groups can be wonderful. However, they can also be toxic. Some of the most vehement enforcers of fiction rules—[cough] crit group Nazis [cough]—are ruling critique groups across the land. Even if they're well meaning, they tend to implement the most paralyzing rules that the typical aspiring novelist will ever encounter. Whatever *always do* and *never do* rules they espouse can seem especially authoritative if the critiquer has had some measure of publishing success. So if Jenny at your critique group has had a novella published in an e-book collection, you'd better do what she says, right? Because she *knows*.

I really do love the crit group environment. It provides a way for writers—who often feel isolated in what they do—to be with people who understand their own brand of strangeness. A great critique group can be extremely beneficial and encouraging. But most writers don't have the experience to understand that these rules and laws are matters of preference. Crit groups are still teaching that these are matters of right and wrong. And that can be exceedingly damaging.

I'm not trying to get you to drop out of your crit group or decide to never join one. But if you hear, "Never do X," or "Always do Y," just nod and jot down a note and realize that they may not actually know what they're talking about. And just because something works for one writer's style doesn't mean it will work for every writer's style—or for *your* style.

Participate in critique groups for the positives they can provide, but don't let a crit group's strident commands bother you too much if you don't agree. Smile and wave. Just smile and wave.

OUR PLAN

This book will liberate you from the perplexities of fiction teaching that can cause paralysis; it will show you how to find your own preferences—your fiction voice; and it will teach you how to use that voice to hook your reader and keep her engaged right through to the end of what you write.

Part One takes you through a number of these issues, looking at the pros and cons and giving my take on each one. We'll look at what you love as a reader of fiction to help you decide what you want to be as a writer of fiction. By the end of Part One, you will have extricated yourself from every bear trap that has been laid for you in the forest that is fiction craftsmanship.

As we've already noted, the typical reader of fiction doesn't give a flip about fiction craftsmanship, high or low. What the end reader wants is to be captured by a story and swept away. So Part Two is about how to engage your reader and keep her engaged right through to "The End." We'll look at craft issues and how they can work for or against engagement, but mainly we'll be looking at the brain chemistry of reader engagement. It's fascinating material and worth the price of this book all by itself, in my opinion.

Part Three looks at some of the most enduring elements of engaging storytelling—from Jung to Campbell to Aristotle. These principles have stood the test of time and will be tremendous assets in your own fiction.

I want to give you license to write the way you want and equip you to grab readers so they not only love your fiction but have to go out and tell everyone to buy it. I want to show you how to write *The Irresistible Novel*. Let's get to it!

Part One
FREE YOURSELF FROM THE PARALYZING RULES OF FICTION

"There are three rules for writing a novel. Unfortunately, no one knows what they are."

—W. Somerset Maugham

I have discovered two books that have helped me tremendously with what you'll find in Part One—and neither is about writing.

The first is an art book: *Finding Your Visual Voice: A Painter's Guide to Developing an Artistic Style* by Dakota Mitchell and Lee Haroun. As an aspiring artist, I wanted to find my own style and voice, and this book was the ticket. The authors took me through questions of inspiration, subject matter, art elements, composition style, and painting process, helping me see the options available and asking which one most appealed to me. It was a fascinating journey, and at the end of the road I knew I was:

> A tonalist who wants to paint dramatic heroic narrative moments depicting strong fantasy/science fiction (SF) characters in forceful or combat poses, depicted in muted, somber tones with high value contrast, a loose brushy look, something interesting with a light source, and lots of broken color and hard and soft edges with evident brushstrokes to create a feeling of dreaminess and sense of the story moment, especially moments in which a smaller hero is standing up to a larger villain.

Who knew?

Now, I don't always paint like that, but it was very helpful in giving me an understanding of what I wanted to be like as an artist. Just as helpful, I think, was realizing that there was no right or wrong answer; my preferences are exceedingly valid, even if not everyone ends up liking my art or subject matter. That doesn't bother me, because plenty of people do like what I'm painting. More importantly, *I* like it.

So it will be with you in finding your fiction voice or style. I'm going to free you to like what you like and shrug off the rest.

There's the age-old question of whether you should write (or paint or whatever else) to please your audience or to please yourself. I don't think it's an either/or question. Think of it more as a continuum, with pleasing only your audience on one extreme and pleasing only yourself on the other. An artist who abandons all sense of himself to chase after what the crowd wants might feel he has lost himself or prostituted himself or sold out. An artist who gives no thought at all to what others will think of his art might be seen as entirely self-centered or just off on some sort of self-therapy safari.

We all have to find our personal sweet spot on this continuum, and that spot may change from year to year or day to day. What I'm doing in *The Irresistible Novel* is helping you find how you'd prefer to write, how it comes to you naturally, and what you like in the fiction you read. Whether you go with those choices, even if they don't mesh with reader preferences—or agent/editor preferences—is up to you and will vary throughout your writing career. But it's powerful to find your style as a writer, even if you sometimes adjust it.

The other book that guided me in the creation of Part One was very different from the first. In *Systematic Theology*, Dr. James Leo Garrett, a professor of mine at seminary, examines pretty much every doctrine in Christianity one by one. For example, on the topic of baptism, he surveyed all the major teachings and positions that Christian groups have held about it over the centuries. He made no judgment among them, and he presented them all fairly. At the end of each section, he gave what he thought and why, but he made it clear—in the book and in class—that any of the views was valid if supported by the rest of the Bible.

There were many, many doctrines I'd never even thought about, much less examined with historical and theological rigor, so it was quite a process. But at the end, I knew what I believed on each one. Even better was that I knew there was a variety of belief on these matters and *that was okay.*

Part One of this book, therefore, is laid out in the spirit of those two other books. We'll look at more than one hundred issues that fiction experts argue about, we'll look at the pros and cons of each position, I'll give you my opinion (at the time of this writing—I'll probably change later!), and then I'll ask you to decide how *you* want to do it.

Where you personally land on each of these issues as you read through this book may not be where you land on them in six months or six years. I certainly went through an evolution in my thinking, and I suspect you will, too. That's okay. But it's empowering to be able to resolve each dilemma and keep moving forward.

WHICH IS IT?

It's possible I may have confused you a bit. I've said that your own preferences as a novelist trump the rules and prohibitions thrown at you by fiction experts. I've also said that keeping the reader engaged trumps everything else in fiction. So which is it?

It's both, of course! When I speak about resolving the dilemma of having or not having a prologue or whether to steer clear of "to be" verbs or not, I am giving you permission to side with whichever option you prefer as a reader of fiction. So your own preferences trump the preferences of others at the level of fiction craftsmanship.

But when I'm speaking at the top level, the level of storytelling and what the reader really wants, I'm urging you to keep reader engagement as the highest goal in writing fiction.

It's possible to make your own choices about craftsmanship and still delight your reader. You can't please every reader, so don't even try. But trust that there are enough readers out there who don't mind prologues or description or *-ly* adverbs to make your novel work out just fine, so long as you keep them engaged.

As you read Part One, keep these words in mind. The rule isn't the thing. Obeying the rule isn't the secret to success—and neither is breaking it. Reader engagement rules all.

YOU AS FICTION READER

Before you begin chapter one, consider reading a novel. Any novel. Not necessarily one you like or have read before. Since you're a writer, you'll probably notice craft issues you've heard someone teach about. You'll notice POV errors and show versus tell issues and wacky speech attributions. You'll notice when the author "gets away with" things you've been told you're not allowed to do. You'll find yourself skipping over certain bits. You might even find yourself loving certain things the author has done.

This is a great exercise to learn about yourself as a reader of fiction. If you find that you hate description of all kinds, that's not right or wrong. It's just what you prefer, and that's okay wherever you land on the matter.

Now give yourself permission to not write description in your fiction. You heard me. If you don't like description as a reader, you don't naturally want to include it in the fiction you write. Why would you include for other readers the very thing you hate as a reader?

I know you may have heard fiction teachers go on and on about how important description is. The chances are good that you're going to hear even more teachers talk about it. So what? I hereby authorize you to leave it out. Leave out everything you hate and include everything you love. Whose book is this anyway? No matter what you choose, you'll be able to do the main thing in your fiction—retain reader engagement—if you follow what I teach in Part Two, so you might as well choose what you like best!

Now, if you're trying to get through a particular publishing gate and the gatekeeper says he won't publish your book unless you add description, then you have that hard choice to make. But if that's not the situation, just leave out what you hate and include what you love. If you do it any other way, the stuff you dislike is likely to be weak and halfhearted, which does no one any favors.

I started out by asking what makes you love a novel and what caused you to first become a lover of story. Go back to that now. Make a list of the things that caused you to become entranced by a piece of fiction and set it as your goal to put that list—and all the other things you love about novels—into the fiction you write.

Chapter 1
PROLOGUES

Since prologues are what begin a novel (well, a novel that *has* a prologue), it's fitting that we should begin there ourselves. Besides, I've seen some whopper arguments over this one, which is always amusing.

THOSE OPPOSED

People who say you should not write a prologue have several reasons for saying so. For one thing, they say readers skip prologues. If you put anything important in your prologue, the reasoning goes, it will get missed and readers will be confused.

Those opposed say that prologues are full of backstory and information dumps (two forms of telling), which are boring to read. The beginning of a novel, when the reader has not become engaged in the story or characters yet, is a bad place to include content likely to bore the reader. It's better to include something *interesting* happening when you're still trying to get the reader on the hook.

Richard Russo, in his Pulitzer Prize–winning novel, *Empire Falls*, begins with a sweeping, historical sixteen-page prologue, in italics, describing events across three generations of a prominent family in the town of Empire Falls. Then chapter one introduces the protagonist and present-day events. The italicized backstory reappears throughout the novel and slowly reveals additional puzzle pieces (while raising more questions!) that build an epic story of an entire town.

It's not the sort of thing that would be likely to engage my brain, but it did win a Pulitzer, so what do I know?

Some say prologues don't have anything to do with the main story. They are filler or a stalling tactic that prevents the reader from getting to what's really important about the book. The most tolerant of these folks can endure a short prologue—but not more than five pages. If you simply must preface the good stuff with something else, they say, keep it short.

Others argue that prologues are added as an afterthought because the author receives some sort of feedback that something isn't explained or working in the story. So the prologue gives a preemptive information dump to address the problem.

THOSE IN FAVOR

Those who love prologues counter that readers actually do read prologues. I have done informal surveys at dozens of writers conferences, asking whether or not the attendees read prologues. The split is almost always 90–10 in favor of those who do read prologues, though the results may be skewed by the fact that those polled are all novelists.

However, the argument that prologues shouldn't be included because no one reads them is not valid. (And if a reader skips a prologue and then complains about being confused, the problem may not be with the novel.)

Those in favor of prologues agree that many prologues do amount to nothing more than information dumps and heaps of backstory. However, that's an ailment (or a blessing, depending on your preference) that afflicts whole manuscripts, not just prologues. If you want to eliminate telling from your fiction, the solution isn't to simply avoid prologues. That's not going to make the telling magically disappear from the whole manuscript. You've got to cut the telling wherever you find it, not only in the opening pages.

In other words, the problem isn't that there's a prologue but that there's telling. If you started with chapter one instead of with a prologue, and if you filled chapter one with backstory and other forms of telling, then the problem would remain.

Those who love prologues say that a prologue doesn't have to be filler or have nothing to do with the main story. The solution, they say, isn't to cut the prologue but to begin the book with something pertinent to the main story.

As for prologues written as a band-aid to fix poor writing later on, the problem isn't with the prologue but with the poor writing later in the book. Go fix that and then ditch the prologue, if that's the only reason you had written it. If there are other reasons for the prologue, then maybe keep it in.

MY OPINION

I'm a big fan of prologues. Let's say your hero is not doing anything especially heroic at the outset of your story, but this is a book of heroic adventure. Let's say, in fact, that your hero is currently a whiny farm boy doing chores with the moisture vaporators and trading power converters with his friends at Tosche Station. I'm just sayin'.

Beginning the novel (or the movie) with that would be downright boring. It probably wouldn't engage the reader at all. But if you began with an action scene showing a big draconian warship overwhelming a tiny little embassy ship, and if you then showed masked shock troops blasting their way forward against plucky, fresh-faced defenders, you'd engage the reader for sure.

Then, with the reader fully engaged, you could introduce the farm boy and go from there. (That was *Star Wars*, by the way.)

A Throne of Bones by Vox Day begins with the Sanctiff (the equivalent of the Pope in this fantasy world) staring at a masterpiece painting that had been hidden in the underground archives for generations and newly rediscovered. The painting, called "Death of the Undying," is of a man who has been stabbed by the six men standing around him holding daggers. But there are seven puncture wounds—one man has stabbed twice. Why? Who? It would all be simply an esoteric exercise if the dead man in the painting weren't the spitting image of the Sanctiff's dear friend.

With this intriguing prologue, the author not only engages the reader but also sets up the chief mystery of the novel: Are there truly immortals among us, and do they mean us harm?

Oh, yes, a prologue like that works very well, in my estimation.

You can also engage if your prologue is humorous, as in this bit from *Hero, Second Class* by Mitchell Bonds:

> Once upon a time, in a faraway kingdom, there lived an old man and his wife. They had no children, and the old man prayed every day that he and his wife would have a son.
>
> This story has absolutely nothing to do with them.

Beginning with a prologue—a scene before our hero is even introduced—can be helpful and effective. So it can be for you if you write a great and engaging prologue. In a prologue you can introduce the villain, set the stakes for the story, establish why the hero is the way he is when the main story starts, show the Big Bad Thing that is coming, and start the time bomb to ticking. Prologues are your friends.

It's not just me, George Lucas, Vox Day, and Mitchell Bonds who have figured out that prologues are a great way to begin a story. I would estimate that upwards of 50 percent of the movies coming out of Hollywood today begin with what amount to prologues. Here are a few you might've heard of: *Pirates of the Caribbean, Frozen, Raiders of the Lost Ark, Atlantis: The Lost Empire, The Fellowship of the Ring, Despicable Me, The Return of the King, Mulan,* and of course, *Star Wars,* just to get the list started.

Now, novels aren't the same as movies, obviously, but if the master storytellers of our age think prologues are a good way to begin a story, it might be something to consider.

TIPS FOR GETTING PAST THE GATEKEEPERS

Writing "Prologue" atop page 1 is a great way to get it rejected by an agent or editor, or marked up in red by a critique group. It's a trigger word like "intolerant" or "inerrant" or "submissive." They don't understand *why* something is considered good or bad; they just have a knee-jerk reaction when they see it. But it's possible to use this lack of understanding to get around this apparent obstacle. The solution is so simple it's laughable.

Don't call it a prologue.

Unfortunately (or fortunately), it's that easy. The gatekeepers and crit group members can be fooled if you simply retitle your prologue as chapter one. If they see no *p*-word, you're golden, even if the opening pages are *functioning* as a prologue. De facto prologues are fine, it turns out. Just don't call them that.

So if you want a prologue in your novel, if you love prologues as a reader of fiction, then put one in your novel. If you feel like living dangerously, you can even call it a prologue. But if you're going to be showing it to agents or editors or critique groups, you might save yourself some grief and just call it chapter one.

YOUR FICTION VOICE

Are you a pro-prologuer or an anti-prologuer? When you read a novel, do you skip over everything that isn't in a "chapter"? Does front matter irritate you? Or is it your opinion that you want to begin reading exactly where the author felt the story began?

There's no right or wrong position on this. Well, the wrong position is the one that finds you including or not including a prologue if you're doing so against your will, better judgment, and preference. I hereby deputize you to include or not include a prologue according to your own inclination.

Fill in the blank: On the whole and for most novels I write, I ____________ begin with a prologue. Though I reserve the right to change my mind for other projects, when it comes to prologues, I'm currently the sort of novelist who ____________________
____
____.

Chapter 2
DESCRIPTION

Description is another element of fiction that people have glorious arguments about.

Apparently, readers, agents, editors, and writers either hate or love description. Complicating matters is the fact that there is a sizable contingent that doesn't care one way or another.

In fiction, description is text that portrays the appearance of characters, items, and locations. "It was a dark and stormy night," while clichéd now, is description.

Description is not the same as narrative, by which I mean the depiction of what happens. "John opened the door" is narrative, while "The room was large" is description. Of course a novel has to have narrative, or we'd have only dialogue in the book. But whether or not a novel has to have description—and how much—is a matter of lively debate.

THOSE OPPOSED

One of my favorite stories about the rules of fiction involves description. I was sitting on a panel at a writers conference in Los Angeles when someone asked whether or not fiction should include description. A few people on the panel gave fairly insipid reasons for or against. Then a novelist took the microphone and said, "I shall never dictate what my reader must imagine."

That answer went over very well. There was applause. It was Los Angeles, after all.

She was voicing what many writers who are opposed to description feel: that description is an intrusion into readers' mind space. If they want to imagine the location looking one way and the author tries to force them to see it another way, it's unwelcome. If readers have pictured a character one way and the author describes him another way, it's almost painful to the brain. That's one reason readers might skip over description.

Another reason they skip description is that it's boring. Nothing is happening. And some authors simply overdo their description, to the point that even those who don't have an opinion about it one way or another become overwhelmed and turned off. I once read a manuscript with four pages describing the clouds. Yes, four pages.

Readers who are also novelists may skip description because they believe that description is telling, not showing. More on that below.

THOSE IN FAVOR

People who love description in fiction can't understand why anyone would want to cut it out. To them, description is the visual part of the book, rather like what shows on the screen at a movie. They don't go to the local cinema to listen to narration only—they go to see things on the screen. So a novel that is light on description is frustrating to them, and they keep hoping for the projectionist to get his act together.

Here's a classic example of description from the opening pages of *The Crimson Petal and the White* by Michel Faber:

> The other, more antiquated houses, despite being two or even three storeys high, exude a subterranean atmosphere, as if they have been excavated from a great pit, the decomposing archaeology of a lost civilisation. Centuries-old buildings support themselves on crutches of iron piping, their wounds and infirmities poulticed with stucco, slung with clothes-lines, patched up with rotting wood. The roofs are a crazy jumble, the upper windows cracked and black as the brickwork, and the sky above seems more solid than air, a vaulted ceiling like the glass roof of a factory or a railway station: once upon a time bright and transparent, now overcast with filth.

People who enjoy description feel that this is how they sense and understand the world and people of the story. If they're not described, the places seem like foggy nebulae and the people faceless and draped in cowls.

There's an adage in theatre that applies here: "If it ain't on the page, it ain't on the stage." It means that if the playwright wants something to be in the play, he'd better write it into the script. If he imagines the scene taking place amidst the wreckage of a steampunk dirigible but neglects to mention that little fact, it's probably not going to appear in the production on opening night.

In fiction, people who love description feel that, if the writer doesn't put the description of something on the page (i.e., in the book), it won't be on the "stage" of the reader's mind. Rather than being passages of description in which nothing happens, these folks counter that much is happening in these passages. The reader's mind is being populated with images, just as if the movie projector finally came on. Telling, which any story can proceed nicely without, is different from description (at least to these people), because if they can't picture where or what is going on, the story can't proceed at all.

MY OPINION

I love description. I can't imagine the scene or the setting or the people unless the writer supplies descriptions of them. As a reader, I despise not being able to picture what's going on, who is there, whether it's inside or outside, etc. For me to be able to enjoy the book, I need to be able to envision it in my head, and for that I need description.

At that panel discussion in L.A., when that writer said she shall never dictate to the reader, everyone clapped, but I was aghast. The author promises to never dictate what the reader should imagine? Really? How is that even possible? The moment the author writes *car* instead of *buggy*, she is forcing the reader's imagination along a very precise path. The moment a character says, "Hello," instead of "Bonjour," the reader's imagination has been dictated to. If the story is set in the year 2001, then the reader has been disallowed from imagining that it's happening in 1066. If the character's name is Jim, the reader has been forced to think of him as Jim and not as Carlysle.

A novel is nothing *but* a precisely guided tour through one story by means of one author's mind and vocabulary and style. Every character who comes onstage, every line of dialogue exchanged, every setting the characters visit, and every item included in the story is an example of the writer selecting this one and not that one, and this one before that one. A novel cannot even exist unless the author "dictates" to the reader what she shall encounter in the book.

When I turn to writing my own fiction, I use lots of description. Not four pages about clouds, but a paragraph or two about every important setting and character in the book. With great description you can not only set the stage for the reader but can also foreshadow, write some very nice prose, and establish the correct mood for the reader as he progresses into the scene.

TIPS FOR GETTING PAST THE GATEKEEPERS

The split between those agents, editors, and critique group members who love description and those who hate description is almost exactly 50–50. The same split exists among readers, as it happens. So what can you do?

You don't worry about it. You write it the way you want to. If you love description, write as much of it as you want. Don't try to second-guess what the agent or editor is going to prefer.

Now, if a gatekeeper says, "You know, I would publish this book in a heartbeat if it had a ton more description," then you're back to that hard choice. Are you willing to put in more (or less) description in order to have a better chance of getting through this gate, or would you rather keep the description where it is and take your chances about finding another gate down the way? Either option is legitimate, and you'll probably find yourself choosing both ways several times over the course of your writing career.

If you decide to put more in, find a good book that talks about writing description well. If the gatekeeper has told you to take out all that description, and you're willing to do so, then just go searching through the manuscript looking to excise your main chunks of description. Either way, keep your original document somewhere safe. You don't want to make these changes, learn that the publisher *still* isn't willing to publish it, and have lost your original.

YOUR FICTION VOICE

As a reader of fiction, do you skip over passages of description? Do you relish those passages? Are you constantly wishing for more description in the novels you read, or do you wish those bits had been cut out long ago?

Are there sorts of description that you like more than others—or that bother you more than others? Perhaps you don't mind bits of description here and there but if you see a paragraph full of it, you'll skip it. Perhaps you hate it when the description is parcelled out over the course of the scene so that it's not until the very end that you learn that the scene took place on the wings of a biplane.

Whatever your preference as a reader, that's how you should do it as a writer. Not everyone will agree with your preferences, but that's okay. When you're writing how you like, your fiction will be stronger than if you were trying to write to someone else's set of preferences.

Give yourself permission to write as much or as little description as you personally prefer.

Fill in the blank: On the whole and for most novels I write, I ____________ use description. Though I reserve the right to change my mind for other projects, when it comes to description, I'm currently the sort of novelist who ________________________
____
__________________ ____.

Chapter 3
-*LY* ADVERBS

The prohibition of *-ly* adverbs (or adverbs of any kind) should be the poster child for the so-called laws of fiction that can leave novelists paralyzed and frustrated.

I don't know if many unpublished manuscripts have been rejected by agents and editors because of the presence of *-ly* adverbs (like *happily* or *strangely*), but I suspect the number is not zero. Certainly it is strike one in the minds of some gatekeepers.

THOSE OPPOSED

Adverbs, especially *-ly* adverbs, are the redheaded stepchildren of the fiction craftsmanship world. When they are hated, they are hated with passion. Adverbs weaken prose, say those who dislike adverbs. It's always better to choose a stronger verb instead of a weak verb plus an adverb. "Walked stiffly" should be replaced by "lurched," they say, and "'Yes,' she said coyly" should be replaced with "'Yes,' she flirted."

Novelists who use *-ly* adverbs to strengthen weak prose or heighten the drama of the moment can produce overwrought sentences like, "He ran rapidly to the quickly closing door and instantly shoved his hand dangerously close to his recently divorced wife and formerly beloved best friend." Ick.

THOSE IN FAVOR

Even those who don't find *-ly* adverbs objectionable would admit they can be overused, as in the sentence above. I don't think anyone argues against the idea of looking for stronger ways to express yourself in fiction, and it's true that *-ly* adverbs can sap strength from prose.

However, sometimes that's exactly (oops) what you want. Dialogue should be exempted from the conversation. Some characters, because of who they are, will use lots of *-ly* adverbs, and others will use very few. Same with internal monologue. *Most* agents and editors, even those who don't like *-ly* adverbs in general, will give you a pass if the dialogue fits the character.

For example, if you're writing dialogue for a proper Brit, who is at pains to be subtle and avoids putting too fine a point on things, he's going to use *-ly* adverbs all the time. "I say, jolly fine day, what? Old boy, if you're not too keenly attached to it, I wonder if you might consider not yodeling so loudly at quite such an ungodly hour of the morning. What do you say, hmm?"

Probably the most egregious effect of the ban on *-ly* adverbs is when novelists earnestly try to avoid using them but come up with something else instead, which results in language train wrecks.

"Yes," he said gravely—er, he graved … ?

"Really?" she asked curiously—um, she questioned.

"I believe so," he said fiercely—uh, he glowered. No, *seethed.*

And instead of "He reached eagerly for the phone" it becomes "He snared the phone" or "He lassoed the phone" or "He tackled the phone." Instead of walking gingerly to the door, he has to limp or saunter or perambulate to the door. And while having him caress her face may be stronger than having him touch her face gently, those in favor of *-ly* adverbs say that it's not a huge difference either way.

Supporters say *-ly* adverbs really do form a legitimate part of the English language. And most, if not all, parts of the English language ought to be fair game for use in fiction.

MY OPINION

I agree that adverbs in general, and *-ly* adverbs in particular, can weaken your fiction. If you're looking for a way to strengthen a given passage, you can look for *-ly* adverbs to replace with more forceful verbs. Also, some novelists do use *-ly* adverbs to shore up sagging prose, and that's probably not a good tactic.

Having said all that, I'm a fan of *-ly* adverbs—as you've no doubt noticed if you're opposed to them and you've read this book up to now. I don't think I overuse them, and I do think I give thought to choosing stronger verbs, but neither do I stress about it. If you want to use *-ly* adverbs, I think you should. If you don't want to use them, it's fine to not use them.

Just watch out for the convoluted positions you can get yourself into by trying to religiously avoid *-ly* adverbs. As an editor and writing coach, I'd much rather see you write "She moved quickly to the door" than "She careened to the door." When you've gone to such an extreme to avoid *-ly* adverbs that the alternative draws attention to itself in a negative way, you're better off with the adverb.

TIPS FOR GETTING PAST THE GATEKEEPERS

If you're publishing straight to the reader (e.g., e-publishing), don't worry about this issue at all. But if you're trying to get traditionally published, you may want to eliminate some or all of your *-ly* adverbs, especially in the opening five to twenty pages.

Aside from the prologue/no-prologue debate, the presence of *-ly* adverbs may be the biggest thing that contributes to getting your manuscript rejected. And as with prologues, the person doing the rejecting may not know why they're bad but has perhaps only heard *that* they're bad. And since *-ly* adverbs are so easy to spot, their presence could be enough to get your book canned.

Despite common perception, agents and editors are not looking for reasons to reject your manuscript. But they are faced with the reality of having seventy-five proposals to get through before the acquisitions meeting at 2:00 P.M., so what they *are* looking for are ways to quickly get through the pile (or should I say, to speed through the pile, ahem). If they're on the fence about a certain manuscript and they spot a handful of *-ly* adverbs on the first couple of pages, that could be enough to cause them to lay the manuscript aside and move on to the next one.

So even if you use *-ly* adverbs throughout your book, you might consider cutting most or all of them out of your opening pages—especially those first five pages.

YOUR FICTION VOICE

Do *-ly* adverbs bother you in the fiction you read? I don't mean, "Has your crit group nailed you so many times about *-ly* adverbs that now you feel you must stamp them out wherever you see them in everyone else's writing as well as your own?" but "When you don't have your critic hat on and you're reading fiction for fun, do *-ly* adverbs bother you?" If they do, then by all means don't include them in the fiction you write.

But if you don't notice, much less become upset by, *-ly* adverbs when you read fiction, don't worry about whether they're going to appear in the fiction you write.

Either way, when you're in edit mode and you're trying to make certain key spots in your book as strong as they can be, one strategy is to go through that passage looking to eliminate adverbs—and adjectives, for that matter—and play with alternative strong verbs and nouns.

The typical reader of fiction has forgotten the meaning of the word *adverb,* so she won't be bothered by their presence in a novel. But prose is subtly stronger (tee-hee) when it has fewer *-ly* adverbs overall, and that subtle difference might be sensed by the reader, even if she can't articulate the difference.

Fill in the blank: On the whole and for most novels I write, I ____________ use *-ly* adverbs. Though I reserve the right to change my mind for other projects, when it comes to *-ly* adverbs, I'm currently the sort of novelist who ________________
____
____.

Chapter 4 PURPLE PROSE AND PAINTED PARAGRAPHS

For many years, I was just one voice among many screaming about how my way was the best and only way to do fiction. I finally took a mellow pill and realized that each of the various alternative theories and methods is fine, and there's no right and wrong—or even best and worst—but simply preference.

One of the key knocks to my noggin that helped me come to this realization was the issue we're looking at in this chapter. I had always held the philosophy of fiction I called "the invisible novelist." In this philosophy, the author stays out of the reader's mind's eye. He strives to keep the prose workmanlike and avoids flowery language. The story and the characters, not the author's impressive wordsmithing, get the spotlight.

I always felt that those "painted paragraphs," in which the author has obviously given excruciating thought to selecting each word, felt too much like he was waving a flag in the reader's face and saying, "Look how clever I am! Bow to my vaunted vocabulary, my sensuous sentences, and my alluring alliteration!"

That turned me off, so for years I urged aspiring novelists away from such purple prose and encouraged them to go invisible ... until I read a sample of an unpublished manuscript by David F. Fry at a writers conference. I was halfway through reading his pages and was all set to tell him to go into stealth mode, when something unexpected happened to me: I suddenly got it. His prose was freaking beautiful, and it didn't take away from my enjoyment of his story in the least. Indeed, it enhanced it, and I wanted to savor every paragraph, not just get through it or mine it for information.

The purple prose I'd seen in the past had been not incorrect fiction craftsmanship but failed attempts at what David had successfully achieved. It wasn't that what they were trying to do was wrong but that their attempts had been inexpert.

And here was the big realization: Even if I didn't want to write this way, I now saw that *it was a valid way to write.*

All of a sudden, I had some rethinking to do. If I was wrong that the invisible novelist philosophy was the only legitimate philosophy of fiction, what other aspects of fiction craftsmanship might I be wrong about as well? Well, not wrong, perhaps, but too adamant that only one way existed.

You can draw a straight line between that moment and this book. So if you end up being helped at all by these pages, especially Part One, you have David F. Fry to thank!

THOSE OPPOSED

Those who are against painted paragraphs, as I've already mentioned, may feel that it is more about the author grandstanding than moving out of the way of the plot and characters. Such painstakingly crafted prose—which is often closer to poetry than typical fiction—is exhausting to read, they say.

The subtext here is that this is literary fiction, and those opposed to painted paragraphs point out that very few readers like literary fiction. Publishers know this as well, so it will be more difficult for a manuscript like this to find a publishing home.

THOSE IN FAVOR

Readers who love the painted paragraph almost don't understand those who don't. For them, it's all about being put under the spell of a poet-novelist's linguistic charms. For them, this is what all fiction ought to aspire to be. Here is an example from Marilynne Robinson's *Housekeeping:*

> Sometimes in the spring the old lake will return. One will open a cellar door to wading boots floating tallowy soles up and planks and buckets bumping at the threshold, the stairway gone from sight after the second step. The earth will brim, the soil will become mud and then silty water, and the grass will stand in chill water to its tips. Our house was at the edge of town on a little hill, so we rarely had more than black pool in our cellar, with a few skeletal insects skidding around on it. A narrow pond would form in the orchard, water clear as air covering grass and black leaves and fallen branches, all around it black leaves and drenched grass and fallen branches, and on it, slight as an image in an eye, sky, clouds, trees, our hovering faces and our cold hands.

Nearly every fan of fiction wants to be swept away. But what exactly we're wanting to be swept away by varies from reader to reader. Some want a never-before-seen world to explore. Some want to live an adventure vicariously. Some want to revisit a beloved era. Some want to meet fabulous new people. Some want suspense that keeps them reading into the night.

And some readers want to be carried away by magnificent prose.

Who's to say that one method of being swept away is right and the others are wrong?

MY OPINION

I will probably never attempt to write literary fiction or even to paint a single paragraph, much less a whole novel. But I have a new appreciation for this sort of gorgeous prose—when it's executed well.

I think it's much harder to write fiction like this successfully. It's certainly much harder to get it published.

It's not my style, but I no longer try to convince other novelists to stop making it their style. If this is what you love in the fiction you read, go for it in the fiction you write!

TIPS FOR GETTING PAST THE GATEKEEPERS

If you want to write beautiful, sensual prose, target only the houses that publish literary fiction. If you send your poetic manuscript to a mainstream publisher, you run the risk of casting your pearls before swine. The editors there (and literary agents as a group) may not understand the merit of what you've done, and it's likely to earn you a rejection letter.

If you're self-publishing this, you don't need to worry. Just paint away.

YOUR FICTION VOICE

When you read the following passage, do you love it or hate it?

> I am sitting here by one of the gurgling brooks, dipping a French water-pen in the limpid crystal, and using it to write these lines, again watching the feather'd twain, as they fly and sport athwart the water, so close, almost touching into its surface. Indeed there seem to be three of us. For nearly an hour I indolently look and join them while they dart and turn and take their airy gambols. ... While the brook babbles, babbles, and the shadows of the boughs dapple in the sunshine around me, and the cool west by-nor'-west wind faintly soughs in the thick bushes and tree tops.

It's a selection from "Three of Us" by Walt Whitman.

If you found yourself luxuriating in the prose, in the limpid crystal and the airy gambols and the faint soughs, you may be a lover of painted paragraphs. If so, you will not be happy unless you're trying to emulate ol' Walt (or the Bard or Fitzgerald or

Mailer). I hereby authorize you to go forth and write in this way without apology.

On the other hand, if you found yourself going, "Oh, come on—give it a rest!" as you read Mr. Whitman, then I hereby give you permission to forget about trying to write this way. Step out of the limelight and let your story and characters shine.

Fill in the blank: On the whole and for most novels I write, I ____________ write painted paragraphs. Though I reserve the right to change my mind for other projects, when it comes to painted paragraphs or invisible novelists, I'm currently the sort of novelist who ____
____
____.

Chapter 5
THE IMMEDIATE INCITING INCIDENT

The inciting incident is the thing that gets the story going. The story world and the characters had been doing X, but then along comes Y, which sets things in motion.

Peter Parker is just a regular high school nerd—until he gets bitten by a special kind of spider, giving him superpowers. The spider bite is the inciting incident in the story of Spider-Man. Without it, you would have no story.

Indiana Jones is just a mild-mannered international archaeological superstar (Go, Indy!)—until he meets with some men from the Department of Defense who tell him that the Nazis have found the resting place of the Lost Ark of the Covenant. Now he's an international archaeological superstar in a mad race for the Lost Ark. The visit from the DOD men was the inciting incident of *Raiders of the Lost Ark.*

The "law" of fiction under debate is whether your novel's inciting incident must appear on page 1 (or, at the very latest, page 20) to get published.

No matter what, I urge you to begin the book with something interesting happening. If not action, then something surprising. As you'll see in Part Two, your reader's brain needs to see one of these two things or it will tell her to keep looking for something else to read. What I'm talking about here is whether you must include *the main challenge of the story* on the opening pages of the novel.

THOSE OPPOSED

People opposed to the inciting incident on page 1 argue that if you bring the inciting incident right away, it has no impact on the reader.

Imagine if page 1 of a novel shows a family sitting around watching television, when a gunman bursts in and shoots them all. The reader, who has had no chance to connect with the characters, might be alarmed by the violence, but when it comes to the death of the characters, all he can probably muster is a shrug and a "that's too bad."

But if you first take a few pages to introduce us to the family, things might be different. If we learn that Heather is pregnant but hasn't told her parents yet, and Micah has gotten a full scholarship to USC and is heading off to school in the morning, and Phillip has been sober for a thousand days, and Louise is secretly checking messages to see if her lover has responded after their argument … then we start getting engaged with them. We start caring about them. So when the gunman bursts in and shoots them all, we feel something. We hurt. We might flinch or even cry.

Those opposed to having the inciting incident on page 1 say they'd prefer to engage the reader than to obey some made-up rule.

Take for instance the story sequence used by the animated movie company Pixar:

- Once upon a time there was ___.
- Every day, ___.
- One day ___.
- Because of that, ___.
- Because of that, ___.
- Until finally ___.

So for the Pixar movie *WALL-E,* it would go something like this:

- Once upon a time, there was a little garbage-cleaning robot who lived alone cleaning up Earth.
- Every day, WALL-E went to work, cleaning up the endless piles of garbage, and came home to his hut.
- One day, a rocket landed and deposited a very pretty girl robot, EVE, whom WALL-E was immediately smitten by.
- Because of that, he spent his days trying to woo her, and he succeeded in doing so—until the rocket returned and took EVE away.
- Because of that, WALL-E hitched a ride on the rocket and went to the space station to try to get EVE back; while there, he encountered the human race, who had grown fat and helpless.
- Until finally, WALL-E managed to win EVE's love and bring humanity back to Earth to be its caretakers once again.

Can you spot the inciting incident? It's not on page 1. It's the line "One day…"

Okay, so, just because Pixar does it this way doesn't mean it's the right or only way to do it. But it does lend support to those who decide they don't want the inciting incident to happen on the opening pages.

THOSE IN FAVOR

You must engage your reader from beginning to end—my great commandment of fiction. Another "rule" of fiction is that you must begin with action in order to hook your reader. Those in favor of having the inciting incident on page 1 cite these as reasons to do so.

After all, what could be a better hook for the reader than the main challenge of the novel? And if you want to hook the reader right away, it stands to reason that you ought to include the main challenge of the novel on page 1.

Despite these arguments, Hollywood isn't doing this. It's actually difficult to find a modern movie that puts the inciting incident at the very beginning of the film. Most of them (and most novels) follow Pixar's approach, establishing the normal—the "Every day, he ____" stuff—before disrupting normal with the "One day, ____" inciting incident.

Some novels and movies that begin with a prologue sort of have the inciting incident on page 1. For instance, the Disney movie *Mulan* begins by showing the villain and his army swarming over the Great Wall of China. In a sense, that's the inciting incident because it's introducing the main challenge of the story. In another sense, it's not the inciting incident because this main challenge has not yet intruded into the hero's life. That happens later, when a messenger from the emperor comes to Mulan's village calling for conscripts into the army.

So if you define inciting incident as showing the main challenge of the story, as I have, then a prologue like that does the trick. If you define inciting incident as the moment when the main challenge of the story breaks into the hero's awareness, then we don't have many books or movies at all that do this.

MY OPINION

If our definition of inciting incident would encompass a prologue that shows the main challenge of the story on page 1—as *Mulan* and *Star Wars* and *Despicable Me* do—then I'm good with it. But maybe that's just because I love prologues. If you want to have the inciting incident on page 1 but you don't do prologues, it's going to be a lot harder to make this work.

However, if we're defining inciting incident as the main challenge of the story intruding into the main character's life, then I'm not okay with presenting that on page 1. As illustrated by our example of the gunman shooting the family watching television, we haven't had time to engage with the character yet, so showing something big happening to this random person would have almost no impact.

That's not to say one is right and another is wrong. It's simply my feeling, my preference, that it's stronger for the kind of fiction I write and more engaging for my kind of reader to establish normal before violating normal. But if this "law" is fulfilled by a prologue that establishes the villain, then I might do it—not to satisfy some arbitrary rulemaker but because I felt the novel could really work with a prologue like that.

I think writing contests—especially those that judge only the first fifteen to twenty pages of a novel—contribute to the idea that you have to start the main story immediately. If judges are reading only fifteen to twenty pages and you take twelve pages or more before the main action starts, or if you don't even have it in those twenty pages at all, they're likely to grade you poorly, even if, in the context of the full novel, that's exactly how the story should be written. Contests provide a sort of artificial insistence on starting the main action right away.

My feeling is that you must surely begin the book with something interesting happening (notice I didn't say "Begin with action"; more on that in chapter eight), but I'm a novelist, which means I'm creative like you, which means I can come up with any number of interesting ways to begin my novel. It doesn't have to show the main action of the story, just as *Raiders of the Lost Ark* began with a scene that introduced the main character and engaged the audience but had nothing at all to do with the main challenge of the story.

TIPS FOR GETTING PAST THE GATEKEEPERS

Agents and editors (and critique group members) will be analyzing your opening pages for something interesting to happen right away. Whatever you decide about where the inciting incident should come or even how to define it, I urge you to begin the novel with something engaging. Whether that engaging bit represents the inciting incident or just some other fun action won't even be discernible until the reader is deeper into the manuscript, so you'll be okay for awhile. Any action at the beginning is better than none.

YOUR FICTION VOICE

I hope you'll begin with something engaging no matter what. But whether your engaging opening is the inciting event or a page of brilliant prose is up to you. If you want your prologue or opening pages to introduce the main challenge of the story, do it!

If you'd rather begin with another interesting bit and spend some time establishing what the world is like before introducing the main challenge of the story, do it that way!

Fill in the blank: On the whole and for most novels I write, I ______________ put the inciting incident on or very near page 1. Though I reserve the right to change my mind for other projects, when it comes to having the inciting incident on the opening pages or not, I'm currently the sort of novelist who __________

____

____.

Chapter 6
"TO BE" VERBS

What's wrong with this sentence: "There were many restaurants in the neighborhood"?

According to those who ascribe to the rule we're looking at in this chapter, it's weak because there is a "to be" verb in it (*were*). They would prefer that the sentence had read, "Many restaurants operated in the neighborhood."

If you travel in fiction craftsmanship circles for very long, you will encounter someone skewering your writing because of "to be" verbs. Every *is*, *am*, *are*, *was*, *were*, *be*, *being*, and *been* will be circled in red, and you will be urged to swap them out for more active verbs.

THOSE OPPOSED

Some say "to be" verbs weaken any sentence in which they're used. They believe, for example, that "I hunger" is stronger than "I am hungry" and that "I doubt" trumps "I have doubts," and that "He arrives," is more forceful than "He's here."

Other reasons to avoid "to be" verbs: They're overly vague ("Spain is great," as opposed to "I love the food and people in Spain."); they are permanent state-of-being verbs when a temporary situation is meant ("I am leaving"—really, you're in a constant state of departure?); and they seem to be statements of absolute truth ("Spanish is hard") when that would not be true of everyone at all times.

THOSE IN FAVOR

Those who like to use (or don't notice they're using) "to be" verbs don't understand what all the fuss is about.

English is founded on the "to be" verb, these folks point out. Our essential questions are *being* questions, like "Who am I?" and "Why am I here?" and "What is life about?" Indeed, perhaps the most famous phrase in the English language is a blatant double use of these: "To be, or not to be?"

And then there's, "I think, therefore I am."

Certainly characters in nearly every novel would use "to be" verbs in their dialogue. Not every one of them would even be conscious of them, much less scrupulous about avoiding them. And think of the effort you'd have to go through to replace every "to be" verb with something else.

MY OPINION

"To be" verbs, like *-ly* adverbs, are a legitimate part of our native tongue and extremely useful (he said, using both "to be" verbs and *-ly* adverbs in the sentence).

Also, as with *-ly* adverbs, sometimes the cure for "to be" verbs is worse than the disease. Instead of, "To be, or not to be," we would have "To live, or to die," which is fine but arguably weaker. By this rule instead of Jesus on the cross saying, "It is finished," we'd have, "It finishes," or something, which is just weird.

But I can't deny that in many cases it is possible (er, the possibility exists) to replace the "to be" verb with something else and thus make it stronger.

What we need is a category of "rules" called "Things to Do When You Want to Improve a Specific Passage in Your Novel." We bring out these tools (I have an editor friend who says he uses tools, not rules, and I like that) when we want to maximize the impact of a given passage, such as the opening half-page of your novel.

Let's say this is how you originally began your novel:

> I was walking down a street I had been down many times before. It was after four, and I was getting hungry. I wanted

> to be with Clarice, of course, but she was in Cleveland and I was in San Diego.

Kind of lame. Now, you could go crazy with eliminating "to be" verbs and end up with something anguished like this:

> I walked down a street I had previously traversed repeatedly. Four o'clock had passed and I hungered. I desired current companionship with Clarice, of course, but she dwelt in Cleveland whilst I resided in San Diego.

Ew, not better. Not stronger. But no "to be" verbs! Sadly, some rule Nazis would consider this an improvement just for that fact. (But then other rule Nazis would pounce on the additional *-ly* adverbs in that version!) How about something a little more creative?

> This street—I knew it well. Nearly four-thirty, and my stomach told me I should pursue food. I wished I had Clarice at my side, of course, but a thousand miles separate Cleveland from San Diego.

Yeah, that may not be great either, but it eliminates the "to be" verbs and still manages to be somewhat interesting to read. It takes more effort to come up with a "to be" verb–free version, but the effort does often pay off.

Would I do this across my entire manuscript? No way. It's a great tool for subtly strengthening key moments in the book, but in my opinion the payoff is not worth the effort of doing it across a full manuscript.

TIPS FOR GETTING PAST THE GATEKEEPERS

In my experience, this isn't an issue that most agents and editors look at. It's more the purview of crit group Nazis. If you show your work at a critique group, I can't tell you how many novelists lash out at other writers for just this sort of thing. Usually it's because that writer got nailed for "to be" verbs or a related minor thing—which became the thing that supposedly prevented him from getting published—

and so now he's on a personal crusade to eliminate all "to be" verbs from other writers' fiction. If he can't use "to be" verbs, no one can.

A multipublished novelist friend of mine received a virulent "fan letter" from a man who had counted all of her uses of *had* in her opening chapters and who proceeded to tell her that ignorance like hers could probably never be corrected and that she had shirked her obligation to the English language.

Yikes—dude, relax.

YOUR FICTION VOICE

Unlike the example above, most readers don't care about "to be" verbs one way or another. Which means you're free to include them or exclude them as you prefer.

Review the most important moments in your book to see if there are "to be" verbs that could be replaced with something more forceful. (Except in dialogue—because characters should be allowed to speak as they would really speak.) If you feel like changing some out, try it. Otherwise, don't sweat it.

Fill in the blank: On the whole and for most novels I write, I ____________ change "to be" verbs to something else. Though I reserve the right to change my mind for other projects, when it comes to "to be" verbs, I'm currently the sort of novelist who ___
____
____
____.

Chapter 7
SHOW VERSUS TELL

Showing and telling, when it comes to fiction, refers to how information is conveyed to the reader. With apologies to everyone named Jim, I like to use this as an example of telling: "Jim was a jerk." That's telling. I simply *told* you that Jim was a jerk.

Showing, by contrast, illustrates or acts something out. So if I were to *show* you that Jim was a jerk, I'd have him come home, kick the dog, stiff-arm the toddler, drop his muddy boots on the couch, put his feet up on the coffee table, and shout, "Woman, where's my beer?"

The "rule" we'll be debating in this chapter can be expressed this way: "Telling is bad, and showing is better; telling will prevent your novel from being published."

THOSE OPPOSED

Telling is the most natural way to write, mainly because it's how we talk. If someone went to a movie you didn't go to, he might summarize it. If your friend comes home from work, she might tell you about her day. Most of our communication is done in the form of summary (i.e., telling), so it makes sense that novelists write this way in their books.

Telling—which is summary—is a whole lot more efficient than acting everything out. I mean, what if you're a honeybee that has to explain to your hivemates where you've found a source of pollen?

You have to act it out for them—this many shakes in this direction for this long of a dance equals direction and distance. That's a lot of work. It's exhausting. How much better if bees had language and the one bee could just say, "Guys, it's right next to the windmill—go!"

Here's an example of telling from *The Eye of the World* by Robert Jordan:

> That was the way of most Two Rivers people. People who had to watch the hail beat their crops or the wolves take their lambs, and start over, no matter how many years it happened, did not give up easily. Most of those who did were long since gone. ... The Congars—and the Coplins; the two families were so intermarried no one really knew where one family let off and the other began—were known from Watch Hill to Deven Ride, and maybe as far as Taren Ferry, as complainers and troublemakers.

Telling is pure exposition. It's summary and narration and explanation. But look how efficient it is. In one paragraph of medium length, you've learned a lot about this corner of Jordan's world.

The end user of fiction—the reader—isn't on the lookout for telling, so it doesn't bother her when she encounters it. Blockbuster-sized bestsellers (not least of which would be Jordan's Wheel of Time fantasies) are chock-full of telling. So obviously writing a book with telling in it does not prevent it from becoming a bestseller.

THOSE IN FAVOR

The question posed by those who prefer showing over telling is whether or not telling is *effective,* especially as it pertains to reader engagement.

Remember Jim the Jerk? When I just *told* you that he was a jerk, did it have any impact on you? At most, you might've shrugged or thought about a jerk in your own life. But you probably didn't feel it. Contrast that with how you felt about Jim after seeing him come home and be abusive. After watching that display, I suspect you were more likely to have felt in your bones that Jim was a freaking *jerk.*

That, these folks say, is why showing is better than telling.

Showing is harder than telling. It takes longer and requires more thinking and creativity. It's usually a broader brush that takes several strokes to convey meaning, whereas telling can be extremely detailed and efficient. Of course, the question isn't which is easier but which is the best way to achieve your goals.

I could tell you that Mrs. Danworth-Myers was turned on by the hero of one of my books, *Operation Firebrand—Origin*, but that's boring and leaves you not even remembering, much less believing, that it's true. But if you watch it happen, it starts sinking into your convictions:

> A man and woman—in their forties, slim, tanned, and exceptionally well-dressed—approached.
>
> "Mr. and Mrs. Danworth-Myers!" Clements said, hurrying to them. "How wonderful to see you. Come to check her out before the reception, eh? Just look at her. Isn't she a beauty?"
>
> "Yes, it's fine," Mr. Danworth-Myers said. "You're sure it'll accommodate five hundred? I don't want anyone left ashore tonight."
>
> "Of course, of course. She's rated for up to 579, not counting crew. And if unexpected guests show up, I'm sure we can find a way to accommodate everyone."
>
> "Well ... we've been thinking that maybe a larger ship would—"
>
> "Come, come," Clements said, leading them onto the boat. "Let me show you the interior. She has two climate-controlled decks, three full-service cocktail bars, and a 2,700 square foot observation deck. Mahogany and brass throughout ..."
>
> Jason shook his head. He unzipped his wetsuit and began to gather his gear. As he did, he felt someone looking at him. Mrs. Danworth-Myers was staring from *The Spirit of Long Beach II*.
>
> Clements appeared again in the doorway. "I'm sorry, ma'am; did you ask about him? Oh, he's just a diver. He works

> for me. Got to keep the ship maintained, you know. Safety is a priority at Sunshine Charters."
>
> She said something softly to Clements.
>
> "I don't know; I'll ask," he said. To Jason he said, "Hey, what's your name, boy?"
>
> Jason considered his answer. Finally he said, "Austin. Steve Austin. My friends call me Stone Cold."
>
> Mr. Danworth-Myers reemerged on deck. "What's going on? Clements, show me the rest of the boat."
>
> "Right, sir," Clements said. "I was just telling your wife about my diver. He's an ex-Navy SEAL, you know. Only the best for Sunshine Charters."
>
> "I don't care if he's a navy blue sea otter. Get back in here and show me the cocktail bar."
>
> "Right away, sir."
>
> Clements scuttled in after Danworth-Myers, but the wife stayed behind, eyeing Jason. She licked her lips and looked him up and down. Jason gathered his gear and made for his pickup, feeling her eyes on him as he left.

I could take five words to convey the information: "This woman is attracted to Jason." But it wouldn't make you feel it for yourself. It took a lot more than five words to get the *feeling* across, but my guess is that it will be more convincing to you this way. I like to say that, when it comes to fiction, all readers are from the Show Me State.

MY OPINION

I am almost 100 percent pro-showing. It is my personal feeling that showing is visual (something our cinema-savvy reader often values), effective for reader impact, and highly engaging for the reader, whereas telling is boring and a momentum killer.

My definition of telling is when you stop the story to explain something the reader doesn't care about. Since stopping the story and making the reader listen to something he doesn't want to listen to both sound like things that could cause him to become disengaged from the book, I personally think telling is a bad idea

99 percent of the time. When do I ever want to kill my momentum and bore my reader?

However, sometimes even I see the need for telling. If a character has been offstage for one hundred pages and we need to know what she was doing but we don't need to see it acted out, then maybe a sentence like this would be warranted: "She recounted how she'd tried to get a permit to fly in their country but had to go to the local municipality, where she'd contracted malaria and spent the summer in the hospital."

My pro-showing soul resists such a thing, but I have to admit that it gives us what we need to know in an effective way. Besides, the thing being summarized was not important enough for us to need to see it all happening as if we were there.

Another good use for telling is the briefing scene. The novel I quoted from above is a military thriller, and in military thrillers you inevitably have that scene in which the commander lays out the mission for the troops. It's essentially an information dump (i.e., telling) scene, but the reader needs it or he will be confused for a long time.

Let's talk for a minute about the so-called "information dump." This is usually described as stopping the story for a sentence, a paragraph, or even a full chapter to simply explain things to the reader. It doesn't move the story forward at all, but it gives the reader everything she needs to know to understand the story.

In my opinion, it also bores the reader silly. It's like having to listen to sweet Uncle Pete, who loves the style of storytelling that reminds one of chasing rabbits for two hours at a time.

I'm not saying that you shouldn't convey information to your reader. A novel is full of information being delivered to the reader. You're constantly setting things up for later and establishing things for the reader. That's as it should be. What I'm talking about in this chapter is the *manner* in which you convey this information. I recommend you do it in a way that makes the reader feel like she's piecing clues together for herself. That's almost always to be preferred over simply delivering it all in lecture or essay form.

I have two criteria for when telling is okay in my own fiction. First, the information has to be revealed or else the story simply can't move forward (like in a briefing scene). Second, the reader has to want to know this information.

So if you start with the information dumping on page 1, that's probably not enough time for the reader to want to know whatever happened to ol' Uncle Clem, you know? But give us a couple hundred pages to wonder what happened to Uncle Clem—Uncle Clem, who was going to return with the life-saving medicines—then, yeah, we might endure a few sentences of summary to let us know.

But by and large in my fiction, I live by this pithy maxim:

Don't narrate—illustrate!

Don't summarize—dramatize!

TIPS FOR GETTING PAST THE GATEKEEPERS

Many agents and editors mention show versus tell issues as a reason for declining a fiction proposal or manuscript.

What is less clear to me is whether what they categorize as telling is *really* telling or something else. Some people confuse description with telling. Some people think any conveying of information is verboten in fiction, which we've already seen is impossible. And others don't see the telling where it exists, as in the famous (but often overlooked) "As you know, Bob ..." error: "As you know, Bob, we are at war with the Ilbanians and we must deliver this document to the commander or risk ruin."

The best way to get past the gatekeepers regarding show versus tell is to simply not tell at all.

You can use this little test I've developed to see if something is showing or telling. Ask this question of the passage: Can the camera see this? If this were happening as a movie or onstage, could we *see* what is being mentioned, or is it all just information given by the narrator?

Refer back to the Robert Jordan passage. Which parts, if any, are happening onstage, and which parts are simply summary? What can the camera see?

It's all happening offstage, invisible to the camera, so it's all telling. (There are exceptions, but this is a good rule of thumb to help you spot telling.)

Keep in mind that, unless a novel is more than 50 percent telling, the end user probably won't care or even notice if there's telling in the book. Put in too much telling, and its inherent ability to bore may become overpowering, but most readers can tolerate much more of it than I prefer. So this process of removing telling or converting it to showing (which you do by acting it out, bringing it onstage) is just to please the gatekeepers.

What you may find in the process, though, is that swapping out telling for showing leaves you with a few spots in the manuscript that you're actually more proud of.

YOUR FICTION VOICE

Do you notice telling in the fiction you read? Does it bother you when the author makes you sit through paragraphs of information on people or topics you simply don't care about? If not, don't worry about converting it to showing in your own book.

Now, you might "worry about it" in the sense of wanting to remove some or all of it from your first fifty pages, since that's what agents and editors will be looking at when they decide whether to accept your work, but you don't need to worry about it in terms of making it an effective novel for your readers. As we've seen, many extremely high-selling novels have lots of telling, so it obviously doesn't bother many readers.

If you don't like telling in the fiction you read, then don't put it in the fiction you write.

It takes awhile to learn how to spot telling in other writers' fiction, and it takes even longer to spot it in your own. The "Can the camera see it?" test will help. Where you do find it, experiment with bringing that "Jim was a jerk" sort of material onstage and acting it out, just to see if you like it better.

You might decide to put showing into the category of "Things to Do When You Want to Improve a Specific Passage in Your Novel." Maybe you don't want to act out everything, just as you might not want to remove every "to be" verb from your whole manuscript. But if you want to strengthen certain key moments in your novel, converting the telling to showing might be just the tool you need.

Fill in the blank: On the whole and for most novels I write, I ____________ choose to work on replacing telling with showing. Though I reserve the right to change my mind for other projects, when it comes to showing and telling, I'm currently the sort of novelist who ____
____
____.

Chapter 8
BEGIN WITH ACTION

In a previous chapter I talked about putting the inciting event of the story in the opening pages of a novel. That's not what we're talking about in this chapter. Here, we're talking about the adage that you must begin your novel with action (even if it's not the main action of the book).

THOSE OPPOSED

While this rule is fairly well-accepted in fiction teaching circles, not everyone agrees with it. What does it mean to begin a novel with action? Usually, car chases and explosions come to mind. Frankly, a lot of novels don't have a single car chase and nary an explosion in the whole book, so then what would "action" constitute?

It could be a ballgame or an argument or a stage performance or someone's death or a mysterious discovery. So long as it strikes the right tone for the novel to come, any of these would be good choices.

But what if the writer doesn't want to begin with anything active happening at all? Must a novel begin with action of some sort? Is there no other option?

We know there are great ways to begin a novel that are not action by almost anyone's definition.

> Call me Ishmael.
>
> Happy families are all alike; every unhappy family is unhappy in its own way.

> It was the best of times, it was the worst of times.
>
> You don't know about me without you have read a book by the name of The Adventures of Tom Sawyer; but that ain't no matter.
>
> It is a truth universally acknowledged, that a single man in possession of a good fortune, must be in want of a wife.

Granted, those are just opening lines, not opening scenes, and those are drawn from novels of yesteryear. But the point remains that it's possible to have a great novel that doesn't begin with a tank blowing up.

What about a novel that begins with the unique voice of the narrator? What about a novel from the painted paragraphs school of fiction?

My fourth novel begins with the hero finding out that he's been assigned to kill someone—but the scene itself consists mainly of thinking and talking, not your typical description of an action-packed beginning.

Also, as you'll seen in Part Two, you don't have to begin with action if you begin with intrigue or surprise.

THOSE IN FAVOR

Those who advocate beginning a novel with action want your reader to be immediately engaged in your book. Hard to argue with that.

The boring beginning, they argue, could prevent your reader from becoming your reader at all. Sometimes I'll read a book's first page—or even just its first line—to see if it hooks me, and if it doesn't, I put it down and keep looking.

Would you keep reading a novel that began like this:

> Ruth had already gone upstairs twice that morning to try to wake Johanna. Both times her sister had grumbled something that led her to believe—wrongly, as it turned out—that she really was going to get up. *Why do I always fall for it, every*

> *single day,* Ruth scolded herself as she climbed the stairs for the third time.

Now, this is the beginning of *The Glassblower* by Petra Durst-Benning, and on the day I wrote this, it was the number one book in Amazon's historical romance category, so apparently it was selling just fine.

But I personally wouldn't keep reading it, and not just because I'm not a fan of romance novels. It's just boring to me. It feels mundane, safe, and even tedious, which is what my life too often feels like as it is. I don't come to fiction for more of that. There's nothing of danger or intrigue here. I would just keep looking.

Would you continue reading a novel that begins like this next one:

> It was a pleasure to burn.
>
> It was a special pleasure to see things eaten, to see things blackened and *changed.* With the brass nozzle in his fists, with this great python spitting its venomous kerosene upon the world, the blood pounded in his head, and his hands were the hands of some amazing conductor playing all the symphonies of blazing and burning to bring down the atters and charcoal ruins of history.

Wow. Well, I personally would keep reading that. It has both action and surprise, both danger and the unexpected. I wonder what in the world is going on, and I feel my brain perk up with all its information about staying safe when around open flame. Apparently, readers have been able to stick with this book fairly well over the years. It's the opening of *Fahrenheit 451* by Ray Bradbury.

Give your reader danger or action or surprise in the beginning, and he'll have a hard time *not* sticking with your book.

Agents and editors are like that, too. They may have sixty-three other proposals they're trying to get through before lunch, and if a novel doesn't grab them right away, they lay it aside and move on to the next one in the stack. Even if the first line or two grabs him, when an agent or editor sees a novel that begins with someone thinking or a description of the clouds or a massive information dump about the history of something, he knows the odds are very good that this book is not going to be a winner.

Readers want to be swept away by a novel. Unless a novel has been recommended strongly by people they trust—or written by someone they're related to—they're not going to give that novel much of their time if it doesn't grab them right away. Starting with action is the most surefire way to engage. The other way to engage is to begin with something unexpected or fascinating happening.

But, as Part Two shows conclusively, it's in your best interest to begin with either action or surprise—or both.

MY OPINION

I don't see any question that the very first line, paragraph, page, scene, and chapter of a novel must engage the reader. She's got a hundred other things she could be doing and a billion other entertainment choices vying for her attention. Your novel has about ten seconds to hook her and maybe two minutes to set the hook. If it hasn't happened by then, you will probably lose her.

Our great commandment of fiction is that you must engage your reader from beginning to end. Well, how can you engage the reader at the beginning?

I'm going to go really vague here, but hopefully it will be helpful: You engage your reader by writing something interesting. (I almost wrote "You engage your reader by writing something engaging," but that would be circular and frustrating. Aren't you glad I didn't write that?)

Seriously, though, you'll find 101 ways to engage someone in a story you want to tell. You can engage through pyrotechnics or poetry, through mayhem or music, through action or anguish. Yes, a car chase or explosion might be engaging, but so might the consumption of a peanut butter and jelly sandwich, if written well enough.

The point isn't what sort of engagement you use. The point is *that* you engage.

If starting with traditional action fits your novel and engages the reader, do it. If starting with nontraditional action, like cracking a safe or finding the last Easter egg, fits your book and engages your reader, it's all good. And if you can pull off an opening that doesn't have action by any definition and yet nevertheless fits your novel and truly engages the reader, then you should do it.

I have begun some of my novels with action, some with nontraditional action, one with a discovery, one with a cryptic discussion, and one with a decision.

In my opinion, the point isn't to begin with action but to engage. However you feel like accomplishing that, either through action or surprise, so long as you do accomplish it, I'd call it a win.

TIPS FOR GETTING PAST THE GATEKEEPERS

As I mentioned, agents and editors are looking for a novel that begins with action. They're hoping for traditional action, willing to accept nontraditional action, and leery of anything else.

That doesn't make it a rule that every novel must begin with action. However, if you're hoping to get published through the traditional route, this is something you need to consider.

If you have begun your novel in a manner other than action, then make this nonaction opening as gripping as possible. You're fighting an uphill battle here, and your professional reader has already given you two strikes (to mix my metaphors), but if you manage to be compelling in your nonaction opening, you can still prevail.

YOUR FICTION VOICE

Pull out the last half-dozen novels you've enjoyed and study their openings. How did they begin? In a variety of ways, I'd guess. Look at the ones that were especially engaging right at the beginning: How did the author accomplish this? Was it traditional action, non-traditional action, or something else?

The point is that it was engaging enough for you to keep reading.

That's what you should go for, too. Because what is engaging for you as a reader will be engaging for other readers like you. Give yourself permission to write it the way you like to read it.

Fill in the blank: On the whole and for most novels I write, I will _________ begin with traditional action. Though I reserve the right to change my mind for other projects, when it comes to beginning with traditional action, I'm currently the sort of novelist who ____
____
____.

Chapter 9
POINT OF VIEW

In fiction, point of view refers to whose eyes we're seeing the story through. There are four primary styles of point of view, though some teachers subdivide these further.

Here are the four traditional points of view (POVs):

- **OMNISCIENT POV:** This is sometimes called head-hopping (though some teachers split hairs about this, mainly over the use of personal pronouns and character voice). Omniscient is when the author may dip inside any character's head and reveal what he is thinking and feeling, using third-person pronouns, plus reveal the past and future. That is why this POV is sometimes called the God POV. Many authors of the classics, including Dickens, used omniscient POV, but it later fell out of favor.
- **FIRST-PERSON POV:** Readers hear from one character, who tells the story using *I*; a line in this POV might be, "I needed to get out of there fast."
- **SECOND-PERSON POV:** This style is almost never used; it's the *you* point of view used in choose-your-own-adventure novels, e.g., "You come to a crossroads; do you turn left or right?"
- **THIRD-PERSON POV:** The author tells the story from the POV of typically one character per scene or chapter, using third-person pronouns like *he, she, him, her,* etc.; a line in this POV might be, "He needed to get out of there fast."

As a general rule, use first or third person. Second-person POV will brand you as a lunatic, and omniscient will mark you as a head-hopping amateur.

THOSE OPPOSED

The best argument against this rule is to point out the many successful novels—including several modern blockbusters—written in omniscient POV.

In generations past, omniscient was the main POV used in novels. Authors like Jane Austen, Leo Tolstoy, and Charles Dickens used it heavily. It's making a resurgence today as well. Modern authors who use omniscient POV include John Irving, Lemony Snicket, Jonathan Franzen, Tom Wolfe, Anne Elisabeth Stengl, and John Updike.

Since novels by some of these authors have been huge bestsellers, we have to view with suspicion the rule that says omniscient is not an acceptable point-of-view style for today.

As for second-person POV, it's hard to imagine it being used for anything except a text adventure or choose-your-own-adventure book. However, *Then We Came to the End* by Joshua Ferris is a very well-known and award-winning novel that successfully uses second-person POV. And, of course, second person is used in things like guidebooks, self-help books, do-it-yourself manuals, interactive fiction, role-playing games, gamebooks, musical lyrics, advertisements, and blogs.

For the moment, having a close, in-mind connection with one or more characters in a story is one of the few advantages novels have over cinematic entertainment. It can't be denied that first person and third person are the most popular styles of POV in use today. But that doesn't mean they're the only possible right choices an author might make.

THOSE IN FAVOR

First- and third-person POV are highly effective, familiar to the reader, and most acceptable to publishing houses.

There's something to be said for writing a novel in a manner that meets the expectations of the reading public. This is akin to the invisible novelist philosophy of fiction. If you go with first or third person (with *I/me/my* or *she/her/hers*), that aspect of your authorship will disappear, in a good sense, because it is what readers expect. That way, you step aside and allow the events and characters of your story, not your authorial hand, to be what the reader notices about the book.

First person and third person are arguably stronger POV styles for building reader engagement with the characters of your novel. While some authors can pull off omniscient in a way that leaves you deeply engaged with the characters, more often than not the author using omniscient POV will leave the reader feeling disconnected. If we're in everyone's head equally, then no one is really our home team.

First and third person bring the reader deeply into the thoughts and feelings of one viewpoint character. It is a disciplined form of POV, since the author must limit herself to only those things that the viewpoint character can feel, think, or know, and in that sense, it takes more strength of mind to keep it limited.

First person, in particular, brings the reader very close to the mind of the viewpoint character. What is more intimate than *I* and *me*? You can't get closer to someone than when you're thinking his thoughts in terms of yourself. If you want the reader to feel especially close to the viewpoint character, consider using first person.

Some say first person went out of style with the alleged death of chick lit or other genres. I say, "Pfft." When someone in publishing says this or that is "out," what she's usually saying is that there have been no blockbusters lately that are like that. All it takes is one giant hit that uses a supposedly "out" style to make it suddenly in. Don't chase trends (that's not a rule, by the way; just a recommendation).

MY OPINION

I'm a big fan of first- and third-person POV. I've used both—and in one case, I used them both in the same novel. (Some agents and editors feel you shouldn't mix the two in the same book, but by now you realize that this is simply preference and opinion held by the gatekeepers.)

In terms of what I have seen in my time as an editor and publisher, omniscient is most often used either by (1) someone who hasn't yet studied the craft of fiction or (2) someone who is writing in the style of yesteryear.

What I don't like about omniscient is that it's much harder to keep secrets from your reader. If you're giving us everyone's thoughts, and if you bring Gladys (who is secretly the murderer in your suspense thriller) onstage in a scene, you're probably going to have to write out her thoughts about where she's going to hide the body, which sort of blows the mystery about the killer's identity. I'm sure there are ways to hide things from the reader even while using omniscient POV; I just don't know what they are.

I have seen some beautifully written and award-winning novels in omniscient POV, so I know it can be done fantastically. So perhaps what I should do is urge novelists to write with first- or third-person POV for their first couple of novels and then branch out to omniscient when they've achieved the level of discipline and expertise required to use omniscient effectively.

Some novels use multiple viewpoint characters, usually in third-person POV, but stick to one viewpoint character per scene. Some of those novels have upwards of a dozen POV characters. Certainly Tom Clancy novels and most epic fantasies do this. It's a great way to give the feeling of a very large event happening, because you're showing it from multiple angles. I do this in my novels, too. It's very useful for thrillers.

But how many POV characters is too many for a novel? I would never give a rule, but for myself, and speaking of viewpoint characters we're going to see again and again over the course of the book, I probably wouldn't go much beyond six. Start having many more than that, and I find that it becomes difficult for the reader to tell them apart or remember which is which.

TIPS FOR GETTING PAST THE GATEKEEPERS

If you're willing to write in first or third person, you almost have no concerns with gatekeepers. Between the two, I'd say the typical agent or editor prefers third person over first person. Still, either one should be fine (unless the gatekeeper you encounter is convinced that first person is dead—in which case, you have a choice to make, don't you?).

Second person will probably just get you laughed at, so maybe save that wildly experimental piece for when you have a great and long-term relationship with a publishing house or a horde of readers who will buy your book no matter how it's written.

Omniscient is tricky. There's probably an 88 percent chance that the gatekeeper who sees it will say it's "wrong" to use omniscient and that the only correct POV styles are first and third, and he will therefore reject your book at the first sighting of a head hop. But if you go to a literary fiction publishing house, or if you just happen to find one of the few agents and editors who like omniscient, you might be okay—assuming you've used omniscient well.

Some agents and editors object to having what they feel are too many viewpoint characters in any given scene or chapter. This is often perceived as a lack of sophistication on the part of the author. Since that is the perception (whether it's true or not), if you're trying to get traditionally published, you might consider limiting the heads you're in for those opening chapters.

Can you mix first-person and third-person POV in your fiction? Some agents and editors will say no—emphatically, even. But it's clearly just preference. I did this in my fifth novel. I was on book two of a trilogy, and I'd done third person only in book one. But I wanted the reader to feel especially connected to a new character in book two, so I experimented with putting her scenes in first person (which feels very intimate to the reader) but leaving all the other viewpoint characters in third person. I never had a single complaint from a reader, though agents might've rejected the book because of it.

This is a good illustration of the idea that sometimes what the gatekeepers teach is not in line with what readers like. However, if you're trying to get this book past those gatekeepers, you might want to avoid revealing the first-person/third-person mixture until chapter four or beyond.

YOUR FICTION VOICE

Before reading this chapter, were you especially aware of POV in the fiction you've read? If not, take a look at some of the novels you've enjoyed and see if they're using *he/him* or *I/me*—and if the author is staying inside one head for the duration of the scene or is jumping around, giving us the thoughts of multiple characters in the same scene.

If you have a preference about POV, or if you're trying to re-create some of the magic you felt with a specific book you loved, then by all means write according to your preference. Of course, if you want to go the traditional-publishing route, you'll need to keep in mind the things I've said about gatekeepers.

If you don't have a preference, then why not take one of your multipage scenes and try it in each of these POV styles? Show all the versions to friends or your critique group to see which one seems to work best or match your overall style.

Fill in the blank: On the whole and for most novels I write, I will use the ____________ point of view style(s). Though I reserve the right to change my mind for other projects, when it comes to POV, I'm currently the sort of novelist who ______________________
____
____.

Chapter 10 SPEECH ATTRIBUTIONS

"Yes," he said.

Speech attributions are the "he said" parts of dialogue scenes.

When you're watching a movie, most of the time it's exceedingly obvious who said what, because you see the person's mouth move and you hear the words come out. But in fiction, you don't have that luxury. Without pinning a nametag onto lines of dialogue, it's possible for the reader to become confused about who is speaking.

Not many people argue about the need for speech attributions in fiction, but rather what those speech attributions should be. Some say you should use only *said* or *asked*, while others say you should avoid repetition and use as many different words as possible, like *opined*, *queried*, *lectured*, *growled*, and *harrumphed*.

The so-called rule here could be stated in a variety of ways, but the one we'll go with for this chapter is, "You should avoid using *said* and *asked* too much and should instead find alternatives as often as possible."

THOSE OPPOSED

Sometimes a problem in fiction arises because the author is trying to adhere to some rule of fiction. If you're not allowed to start with a prologue, for instance, some authors will resort to flashbacks, which is arguably worse. If you're not allowed to use *-ly* adverbs, some authors will come up with some awkward wordings. Efforts to avoid one pitfall can cause you to topple into another.

That may be the case with speech attributions. If you've been told to avoid repetition, and especially to avoid the repetition of certain favorite words or phrases, you'll find that you use the word *said* over and over and over. Thousands of times in the book. Ack!

So you might change this one to *shouted*, that one to *wondered*, and this next one to *guessed*. Pretty soon, the thesaurus comes out, leading to, "'Yes,' he interrogated," and "'Yes,' she harangued," and "'Yes,' they avowed." Then those run out, and the author gets creative. "'No,' she managed," and "'No,' she sighed," and "'No,' she fretted." But there are still not enough words to avoid repetition. So out come the really fun ones, like, "'Wait,' she admonished," and "'Wait,' she conjectured," and "'Wait,' she authorized." And let's not forget my favorite: "'I'm sorry,' she apologized."

In an effort to avoid one supposedly bad thing—the repetition of *said* and *asked*—you end up doing something arguably worse.

This is sometimes an issue of which philosophy of fiction you subscribe to. If you're going with the painted paragraphs philosophy, then showing off your creative replacements for *said* and *asked* might be just what you're looking for. If you subscribe to the invisible novelist philosophy, then *said* and *asked* are perfect because they are invisible to the reader. It's when you get creative with "'Yes,' she intellectualized," that it becomes distracting.

Surely not every word is objectionable even if used over and over in a manuscript. We don't hear anyone saying you must avoid repeating *the,* for example, or *and,* yet those words appear tens of thousands of times in a book. So it's not actual repetition that is the issue but repetition of certain words.

Another reason given for replacing *said* and *asked* is that they sometimes lead to the use of the dreaded *-ly* adverb. Why use *said* if it's going to result in a *said loudly*? Why not go with *shouted* and call it even?

It's certainly a matter of opinion, but some people would rather read an *-ly* adverb than be told that someone has just queried a question.

A great way to get around the whole matter is to use beats in place of attributions.

> "That's terrific!" Julia sat on the ottoman. "When do you start?"

There's no speech attribution here—no "'That's terrific!' Julia said"—and yet we know it was Julia talking.

Beats are your friends for a number of reasons. First, as we've seen, they can replace speech attributions while nevertheless performing the same function. You don't need: "'Yes,' Jim said. Jim sat on the sofa." You can write simply, "'Yes.' Jim sat on the sofa," and accomplish the same thing but with fewer words.

Second, beats tie the reader to the setting. Having Jim sit on the sofa centers us in that location. By giving these bits of stage business and by reminding us of people or things in the environment, you tether us to that reality. Without beats, a dialogue scene becomes a case of floating heads in which the conversation loses all grip on the land and drifts into a netherspace we can neither picture nor remember.

Third, beats are your primary tool for managing the rhythm and pacing of your dialogue scenes. Let's say you imagine a long pause between these two lines of dialogue:

> "I'm having a baby."
>
> "Oh, really?"

As you read this, did you *sense* a long pause between those two lines? Probably not. To the eye, the second line appears to come right on the heels of the first. But now read it with a beat:

> "I'm having a baby."
>
> Thomas felt as if a trap door had opened beneath him, dropping him toward the earth far below. The room spun, and he found a chair and managed to sit. He looked at Sylvie's face.

> Was she pulling his leg? Didn't look like it. "Oh," he said, trying to sound rational, "really?"

Maybe I overdid it for emphasis, but my guess is that you *felt* a pause this time. Another beat even inserted a pause between *Oh* and *really*.

Use beats in dialogue scenes as an alternative to some of your speech attributions and as a Swiss Army knife for your writer's toolkit.

Whatever you decide about your primary way of dealing with attributions, I recommend you use beats much of the time.

THOSE IN FAVOR

Those in favor of avoiding *said* and *asked* point out that a repeated word or phrase can be distracting to even casual readers. For example:

> Charles was lucky that luck was with him. Julia was as unlucky at cards as she was at love, but whether it was the luck of the draw or the luck of the Irish—or just plain dumb luck—Charles had it, and for that fact, he regularly thanked his lucky stars.

See? Not so nice. You're lucky I didn't continue (ahem). Even the overuse of a character name can become annoying to the eye:

> Ronald liked playing video games. The Mass Effect series was Ronald's favorite, and every time Ronald had friends over, that was the game Ronald wanted to play. Ronald's mother tried to get Ronald to expand his interests, but what could she do? Ronald was forty, and Ronald knew what Ronald liked.

Yeah, you get the picture.

There's no question that such repeats should be avoided, or at least toned down, in fiction. But the question remains, where do you draw the line? Folks in favor of this rule say that *said* and *asked* clearly fall on the wrong side of the line, and so they crack open the thesaurus and replace those words, and the clunky *-ly* adverbs that often accompany them, with *challenged*, *explored*, *theorized*, and *excoriated.*

Others say they like to change out *said* and *asked* just to add variety. Certainly you shouldn't be restricted by your attributions, even if you choose to stick with *said* and *asked* most of the time. After all, sometimes people really do shout and whisper, so the novelist ought to be allowed to say so.

MY OPINION

I'm a fan of *said* and *asked*; I ascribe to the invisible novelist school of fiction. *Said* and *asked* are as unobtrusive as *the*, *and*, *or*, *I*, *you*, *a*, and *he*, so I use them aplenty.

However, I think you ought to use as few speech attributions as possible to keep the reader oriented. I also love the use of beats to replace speech attributions. I use all of the above techniques and words, though I stick mainly to *said*, *asked*, and the use of beats.

I'm all for variety and the fresh turn of phrase in fiction, but I'd rather not draw the reader's focus away from the characters, events, and dialogue of the book.

TIPS FOR GETTING PAST THE GATEKEEPERS

Not many official gatekeepers (agents and editors) I know would reject a book if it used—or didn't use—*said* and *asked*. Mainly where you catch flak about this is in the critique group circle. *Said* and *asked* are easy things to mark up if someone is desperate to find contributions to make to the group.

YOUR FICTION VOICE

The typical fiction reader isn't going to notice your use of *opined* vs. *said*, so I think you ought to use them or not as you wish.

What I want you to do is decide *for yourself* if you want to go with one approach or another, and not be swayed by someone who portrays this as an unbreakable rule. What's important, what communicates to the reader, is the *content* of what your characters say, not what language is used to frame it.

Fill in the blank: On the whole and for most novels I write, I will use ____________ for speech attributions. Though I reserve the right to change my mind for other projects, when it comes to speech attributions, I'm currently the sort of novelist who ______
____
____.

Chapter 11
OUTLINING

Are you a plotter or a pantser?

Translation: Do you outline your story before writing it, or do you just take a flying leap, start writing, and figure out what you're doing after you've done it? Do you plan it out, or do you write by the seat of your pants?

The rule we're talking about here could be expressed in a couple of different ways, but we'll phrase it this way: "You must always outline your novel, or it will be doomed."

THOSE OPPOSED

Some novelists are just not plotters. For these folks, outlining kills the creative act. You might as well tell them exactly what they're going to write and how to write it and then expect them to feel like their creativity is on fire when they write it. Not going to happen.

These folks sail onto a blank page like a devil-may-care freebooter and plunge themselves into a story, riding every gust of wind, changing course with every shift in the current, and exploring every estuary that presents itself. To them, writing is about *discovery.* If they think too much about what they're doing, they'll lose the muse, and then they'd might as well lay the pen down, because nothing authentic is going to happen.

Of all the short fiction I've written, my very favorite was written this way. I had an image in my head: a fantasy creature walking on a forest trail I knew. So I just started writing. The creature led me to a civilization of creatures. They had a terrible problem, which led me to speak with the king of the realm about it. I had no idea where the story was going—or, more accurately, where it was *coming from*—

but I didn't care. I had a tiger by the tail, and I was determined to hold on until the end. It felt like I was having a vision or was able to chronicle a dream. And when the king gave his reply, I felt it in my toes. This was the right answer, the ultimate answer.

The experience was about discovery, but it was self-discovery. I've never been able to replicate that feeling, but it was amazing, and I can see why writers love this approach to fiction.

THOSE IN FAVOR

The plotters prefer a feeling of order and assurance that this story is going to go where they want it to go. They know, or at least sense, that a story with no structure can end up as a five-hundred-page meandering mess that may have to be jettisoned entirely.

Plotters, whether they use detailed outlines and charts or are content with a simple three-act structure, like to keep the story on a leash. It's great to explore the creative possibilities that arise serendipitously during writing, but they remain within the parameters of the story they set out to write in the first place.

The pantsers (those who write by the seat of their pants) want the story to find *them* and to be told by the characters where the story should go. The plotters already know the story they want to write. Their challenge is to make it end up the way they envisioned in their head beforehand.

MY OPINION

I'm a hybrid plotter. I like a good plan and a solid three-act structure. But I also love the discoveries and new ways of accomplishing my goals that arise during the writing of a novel. My outline is flexible enough to allow those detours or for Character B to accomplish what I originally had Character A doing. That way, I get the best of both. I get structure, but I can also follow the muse.

Is it possible to underplot or overplot? Sure. If you need some structure but you don't give yourself enough, you may find yourself adrift without a compass or a heading. And if you give yourself too much structure, you can suck the joy out of the writing process.

This happened to me. Years ago, I had this great idea for a novel. I had read some teacher who said I had to plot everything out in detail on index cards. So I did it. In the days before I had children or pets (or a decent spreadsheet program!), I covered the entire living room floor with like five packs of index cards. I had everything on those cards, from large plot points to character tics to great lines of dialogue. I could move whole groups around to reorder the scenes. Finally, I had it all arranged the way I wanted it.

The only problem was that now I didn't want to write the book. I'd made all the fun little discoveries in the index card process. I'd sucked the cream out of the Twinkie. Now all that was left was the grueling task of writing a really long story, but I was tied to the rails of the cards I'd written out.

I never wrote that novel. My overplotting killed it.

Now I am careful to give myself just enough plot to make sure I actually hit my objective but not so much that I'm left with only stale Twinkie cake to eat.

I also outline because I know I'm going to lose objectivity about the story I'm writing. So before I begin, back when I *am* still objective about the story, I craft a (loose) outline that includes all the cool things I really wanted to include. I may end up achieving them in ways I hadn't anticipated, but at least I'll have a guide to let me know what I wanted to achieve.

TIPS FOR GETTING PAST THE GATEKEEPERS

A gatekeeper won't be able to tell whether you outlined your book or were able to just wing it the whole way. So long as the finished result is good, who cares how you got there?

Two caveats, though. First, the pantser is much more likely to end up with a novel that kind of doesn't go anywhere, feels aimless, and may or may not adequately resolve. If you don't know where you're going, you may not know if you got there. And that sort of directionlessness *is* something an agent or editor will be able to detect. Even the pantser purist would do well to have at least a basic understanding of where she wants to end up in the story.

Second, the plotter is much more likely to care about plot than character, leading to a plot-driven book in which the characters are all stereotypes. I've written an entire book on this subject, *Plot Versus Character*, so here I'll say only that plot work is great but cannot be a bulldozer for characters.

YOUR FICTION VOICE

Which do you naturally find yourself doing, plotting or just diving in? Both are right for different people. And even if you're naturally one thing, that doesn't mean you can't gain a bit of help from the other camp. Writers need a nice balance between plotting and discovering, between laying rails and going off the rails.

My main objective with this chapter—with all of Part One, actually—is to get you to see that it's okay to write the way you feel inclined to write. Some fiction expert may claim that you can't do it that way, but you don't have to listen to him (unless he's a gatekeeper whose gate you really, really want to get through).

When it comes to plotting or pantsing, the important thing is to find the method that best unlocks your creativity and gets the story onto the page.

Fill in the blank: On the whole and for most novels I write, I will ____________ my plot. Though I reserve the right to change my mind for other projects, when it comes to outlining, I'm currently the sort of novelist who ________________________________
____
____.

Chapter 12
THAT

This one borders on the ludicrous. Some fiction teachers (and their zealous followers in critique groups) say that you must ban the word *that* from your fiction if you want to be taken seriously as a writer.

The word must go, they say, from sentences like this: "I didn't know that you had come home already." These earnest people point out that the sentence would work just fine without it, becoming: "I didn't know you had come home already." If it can be removed without hurting the sentence, they say, then it should be removed.

THOSE OPPOSED

If a word is a legitimate part of the English language, some writers say, it ought to be fair play to use in a novel. Eliminating a word—specifically one word over all others—because it is sometimes superfluous seems a little silly, these folks argue.

That, like *-ly* adverbs, "to be" verbs, or *said* and *asked,* is easy to spot in a manuscript, so the critiquer looking for something to contribute might latch onto the idea that it should be eliminated. "You might want to remove all your *that*s. It could improve your book, so I marked them all for you. I heard tha—Er, I heard ... you shouldn't use it."

That is a very useful word for providing clarity to the reader. It's also how we speak.

But even those opposed to eliminating *that* from their writing entirely are likely to admit that removing it from certain key moments can be a way to strengthen those moments.

THOSE IN FAVOR

If removing *that* from key moments in a novel makes those moments stronger, why not make your whole book stronger and remove the word altogether?

Most folks who want to remove *that* to strengthen a novel will allow the word to remain in dialogue or direct thoughts. Some characters really would use *that* in their speaking or thinking, so to remove a word they would use to obey someone's rule of fiction might be taking things too far. If all your characters speak with perfect English, and if you're not writing a novel peopled only with grammarians, something may feel unrealistic about the book. Tossing in some "wrong" verbiage in order to gain a feeling of authenticity might be just the ticket.

Even if the crit group Nazis zap you for it.

MY OPINION

Sometimes *that* is just the right word, in my opinion. If you are an anti-*that* person, you've no doubt noted my many uses of the word in the book so far. Sorry for your pain.

My opinion is that if you want to use the word, you should. I will sometimes go through and eliminate some instances of the word as I edit, but most of the time they don't catch my eye, so I leave them alone and don't worry about it.

Sometimes, removing *that* can make the sentence more awkward. "No one told me I was supposed to do." Do what? Okay, maybe only the purists would remove *that* from such a sentence, but even changing, "I didn't realize that I was supposed to call" to "I didn't realize I was supposed to call" feels a little klunky to me.

But, and this is the point, maybe that is just my preference.

TIPS FOR GETTING PAST THE GATEKEEPERS

A handful of publishing gatekeepers, along with lots of critique group participants, will ding you for using *that*. If *that* is something that will bother you, I recommend that you seek to cut down on your uses of it, at least for the opening thirty to fifty pages of your book.

(Seriously, try to write that sentence without the word *that*. Okay, I digress.)

Most of the time, publishing professionals won't be bothered by your use of *that*. Like so many of these topics, maybe seek to limit use of the word, especially in key passages. But on the whole, I wouldn't worry about this word messing up your chances of getting published.

YOUR FICTION VOICE

Go back through some fiction you've written and spot how often you use the word *that*. Does it bother you? Or perhaps you're acutely aware of your use of the word—probably because of someone nailing you for using it. Does the word truly annoy you now, or are you just smarting from the injury done to you?

If the word doesn't bother you, and especially if you use it yourself in conversation, give yourself permission to use it in your fiction. But if the word really does make you cringe, not because of what someone said but because you honestly feel eliminating it strengthens your prose, feel free not to use it.

But whichever you choose, you can maybe give a bit of grace to those who choose a different path. The reader really doesn't care about … that.

Fill in the blank: On the whole and for most novels I write, I ____________ the word *that*. Though I reserve the right to change my mind for other projects, when it comes to *that*, I'm the sort of novelist who ____
____
____.

Chapter 13
SWITCHING BETWEEN STORYLINES

You've probably seen a novel that introduced twelve viewpoint characters and plotlines before you reached page 10 of the book—or lots of little scenes designed to intrigue and engage and show the scope of a book.

Some teachers say you shouldn't do this. They say that the very thing designed to engage readers actually has the opposite effect. So let's examine the rule that says, "You should not introduce a lot of viewpoint characters and storylines very early in a novel."

THOSE OPPOSED

In certain genres like suspense thrillers, multiple storylines and viewpoint characters are their bread and butter. Intercutting between them goes straight from interesting thing to interesting thing in the plot and skips all the dull parts. If this intercutting will be done throughout the book, why not start it on page 1? This shows the scale of what's going to happen in the story.

Besides, maybe storylines one through four don't engage the reader but storyline five does the trick. In that case, it's a good thing all those storylines were introduced right away, or else the reader would've remained unengaged.

THOSE IN FAVOR

If you introduce many storylines and viewpoint characters early in a book, the reader doesn't know who the main person is. She doesn't know where to put her suitcases down, so to speak. Which of these people is going to be my "person"? They don't know, so they can't connect—and if they can't connect, maybe they stop reading.

These writers prefer introducing the main character very early in the book (either on page 1 or after a prologue), then staying with that character's storyline for twenty-five to fifty contiguous pages before cutting away to another viewpoint character and storyline.

This doesn't mean there can't be anyone else onstage with the protagonist during those pages. Indeed, even other viewpoint characters can be onstage in those pages, but we don't see through anyone else's eyes.

Allowing the reader to spend this much time in the protagonist's mind and life, these folks say, gives him time to build those connections every reader is desiring to build. It also gives him a strong fix about whose story this is going to be.

You can still cut away to other storylines, even if you start like this. You can have as many other viewpoint characters and storylines as you want, these writers say, so long as you first clue your reader in on who is going to be the home team.

MY OPINION

I used to believe that staying with the main hero for the first contiguous forty pages of a novel (after a prologue, if any) was the only right way to write. I've since mellowed.

A little.

As you know, I love prologues, so most any novel I write is going to have one of those to start the book. I consider a prologue a freebie, a teaser, that can engage the reader even before the protagonist steps onstage.

But the very next thing I do is introduce my primary hero. And as soon as I introduce my hero, I stay in her head for a good long time before cutting away to another storyline and viewpoint character.

That's not to say that it can't work to start with several vignettes or even chapter-length segments that introduce multiple viewpoint characters and storylines in the opening twenty-five to fifty pages. On the contrary, it's done all the time, and done well. That's just not the most effective method for hooking the sort of reader I target.

Or maybe I should say I don't think it's the most effective way to hook a reader like me. And maybe that's the real issue.

TIPS FOR GETTING PAST THE GATEKEEPERS

Most gatekeepers aren't going to have an opinion either way. They, like readers, are going to like what you've done if it engages them, and they're going to not like it if it doesn't.

YOUR FICTION VOICE

Take a survey of the novels you enjoy the most as a reader and see if there is any pattern when it comes to how many storylines and viewpoint characters are introduced early on.

My hunch is that the way it occurred to you to begin your novel—with several short scenes featuring different protagonists or with a longer sustained sequence following one protagonist—is the way you like to see in the novels you read.

When you identify your own preference as a reader, go with it as a writer.

Fill in the blank: On the whole and for most novels I write, I am going to begin by ____________. Though I reserve the right to change my mind for other projects, when it comes to introducing storylines and viewpoint characters at the beginning of a book, I'm currently the sort of novelist who ______________________
____
____.

Chapter 14
FLOATING BODY PARTS

> His deep green eyes separated from the crowd and moved toward her.
>
> Her heart fell from her chest and dropped to the floor.
>
> Tired feet took him all the way across town.
>
> Her eyes held his face, his hands, his physique.

Yeah, these. We'll phrase the rule this way: "Never let body parts do what body parts can't really do or go where they can't really go."

THOSE OPPOSED

If something is a convention of a particular genre, then the writer ought to do it, even if some people think it's odd. And floating (or "disembodied" or "breakaway") body parts are a convention in the romance genre in particular, and probably a few others, so they should be allowed in those arenas, if not everywhere else.

Also, it's silly to ding an author for some technically impossible figures of speech but not others. For instance, a novelist in any genre can write, "She rolled her eyes," and not worry that the reader will think the character plucked her eyes from their sockets and bowled them across the carpet. If he rakes his hair, (almost) no one pictures a garden rake. As for those tired feet that carry the person across town or the jaw that drops to the floor or the heart that leaps into the person's throat … come on, give me a break. *You know what I mean.*

Some people, writers or not, have fun with hyperbole. If a character being surprised is enjoyable to write (or read about), then maybe having her eyes spring right out of her head is even more enjoyable. Fiction isn't real life, after all, but *heightened* life. Many characters are larger than life, and many novels chronicle events that are well beyond ordinary. So why can't the language in a novel be a little heightened, too?

THOSE IN FAVOR

It's not so much that eyes don't really *hold* someone's face (ew) or that hearts can't really be worn on a sleeve that's objectionable. It's that such language reeks of amateurism or bad romance novels. Of trying too hard. Of gushing. Of the writer apparently believing that his normal language isn't powerful enough alone, so it has to be propped up with ridiculous hyperbole.

Does his heart really need to burst from his chest, or can it just pound? Do her eyes really need to float over the crowd and land on her lover's face, or can she just look around?

If you're not writing romance or maybe a novel from a child's perspective, and especially if you're trying to write according to the invisible novelist philosophy of fiction, then such language is to be eschewed.

MY OPINION

I am not a fan of this sort of writing. I find it syrupy and overwrought.

Then again, that's just my preference. It may also be a reflection of the genres I write in. If my military science fiction had characters whose lungs refused to exhale, it wouldn't be an expression of longing, it would be a description of a malfunctioning spacesuit. Those characters wouldn't be tasting the bittersweet nectar of love—they would just die.

And if I tried to write a romance and I *didn't* use this sort of language, my readers might not be pleased. (Well, if I tried to write a romance, readers wouldn't be pleased by a number of things, but I digress.)

I used to think it was *wrong* to write fiction using floating body parts, but now I think it's just a matter of opinion, like so much else.

I've seen writers purge their own writing—and, especially, the writing of anyone they have the opportunity to critique—of every figure of speech that might even come close to a floating body part. No eye rolling, no heartbeat skipping, and no minds winging their way to faraway dreams.

But where do you draw the line? Is it that all figures of speech are to be forbidden? You can't shuffle your feet, because there weren't fifty-two feet in the deck. You can't count the minutes unless they are actually tallied on a ledger. Is that what we want? If we were to begin exploring how much of our language is metaphorical, we'd be left with only the driest sort of data words, and I can't see how that would be a good thing.

Write your fiction in the way it comes to you, at least in the rough draft. If you later decide to remove the floating body parts or your more colorful turns of phrase, or if you feel that doing so will better communicate to your target reader, then do so. But if you like it with hearts soaring and eyes gluing, I hereby authorize you to keep it that way in your fiction.

TIPS FOR GETTING PAST THE GATEKEEPERS

Most agents and editors won't care about floating body parts one way or another. It's usually just the critique group patrol who will get you for this one. Now, if you're using a lot of these images in a genre where they don't usually occur, or if you're using too few of them in a genre that usually has them, you may be asked to adjust. But for the most part, I doubt you'll find this to be an issue.

YOUR FICTION VOICE

Does this sort of imagery occur to you regularly when you write? If so, that's a good indicator that you like them. Just go with it.

If you don't often find these things coming to your mind for your stories, don't worry about it. Don't put more in if they're not how the story comes to you. They might end up looking like happy face stickers decorating an executioner's hood—not really what you were going for.

Fill in the blank: On the whole and for most novels I write, I ____________ incorporate floating body parts. Though I reserve the right to change my mind for other projects, when it comes to floating body parts and other word pictures, I'm currently the sort of novelist who ____
____
____
____.

Chapter 15
GERUNDS, PARTICIPIAL PHRASES, SENTENCE FRAGMENTS, BEGINNING WITH CONJUNCTIONS, ENDING WITH PREPOSITIONS, AND PASSIVE VOICE

Let's tackle a few of these at once, since they're all flavors of the same ice cream.

A gerund is what you get when you turn a verb into a noun by adding *-ing.* So *defuse* (which is a verb) becomes the noun *defusing,* as in, "Thanks for your defusing of the bomb" and changing *give* to *giving,* as in, "The giving of alms is kind."

I've actually had a very successful novelist tell me that the lack of gerunds is the secret to this person's success. We'll talk about them in a minute.

Some fiction teachers say sentences that begin with participial phrases should be removed altogether. For example, "Having grown up in Cleveland, Jim was a fan of the Cavaliers," or "Screaming loudly, Jenny moved her hand away from the stove."

Sentence fragments are grammatically incomplete sentences. Like this. See how it doesn't have a subject and a verb and express a complete thought? Perhaps in an effort to vouchsafe the English language, some teachers recommend not using them. Ever.

And beginning a sentence with a conjunction is said by some to be an unforgivable sin.

We've also heard that it is verboten to end a sentence with a preposition. So "Who are you riding home with?" is to be rewritten as "With whom are you riding home?" It was precisely this sort of priggish correction up with which Winston Churchill would not put.

Passive voice is when you make the object of an action the subject of the sentence: "A bar was walked into by a priest" or "The fish was caught by the angler." Passive voice, as the name implies, seems to some fiction teachers to be, well, weak and passive, too milquetoast for anyone who desires to write strong fiction.

The rule we'll address in this chapter is in the form of a negative: "Thou shalt not use gerunds, sentence fragments, passive voice, sentences that begin with participial phrases or conjunctions, or sentences that end with prepositions."

THOSE OPPOSED

On all of these, similar arguments will be used pro and con, so it's convenient to discuss them together. Much of this can be understood as the difference between formal writing and fiction writing, or between old-school grammatical advice and modern informal usage—or between what your English teacher taught you and how you'd rather express yourself.

Proper grammar falls into the category of things the average reader doesn't notice or care about. Most readers don't even know what these things are. (I had to look up gerunds, as you can probably tell from my using of them [grin].) Even if the reader would otherwise know what these are, if he's hooked by your story, he won't be bothered.

In dialogue, especially, if characters would talk using these grammatical choices, then by all means they ought to be allowed to do so. Those who try to make an uneducated character speak in perfect English, in order to preserve the sanctity of correct grammar, have missed the entire point of fiction.

Fiction is supposed to be fun. It's a form of entertainment. It should be a place of experimentation, too. *And* it can be a place for informality and style. The voice of the author and the characters ought to be fully heard, even if it would nearly give Old Mrs. Grammarian a heart attack.

THOSE IN FAVOR

The English language has become a travesty. With words like *twerking* and *Googling* and *Skyping* entering into conversations with increasing frequency, and with participles being derived inappropriately from innocuous nouns left and right, English is in a state of apocalypse, and if it does not fall to writers to combat this catastrophe, to whom does it fall?

Granted, some of these are not grammatically incorrect. Passive voice isn't wrong; it's just weak. There's nothing technically improper about beginning a sentence with a participial phrase. Different subgroups oppose the use of some of these but don't have a problem with others, and vice versa. But they are all united in saying that *avoiding* these constructions will improve your fiction. Perhaps they should all fall into the category of "Things to Apply at Key Moments in Your Story."

MY OPINION

I'm all over the map with these, and I hope you give yourself permission to be the same way.

I personally despise sentences that begin with participial phrases, but that's just my preference. And I'm a huge fan of sentences that begin with conjunctions, as you've no doubt seen. Same with sentence fragments. I agree with Churchill, so I don't mind letting prepositions being what I end a sentence with. As far as passive voice, I don't think I use it much, but maybe I do. And what in the world is a gerund? I mean, really.

Those are my preferences right now. What are yours?

TIPS FOR GETTING PAST THE GATEKEEPERS

You have no way of anticipating which of these issues, if any, a given agent or editor will have a beef with.

If that's the case, you might as well not worry about them. Just write the way you want, and if you get feedback saying your book would be given the green light if you were to fix your [whatever grammatical issue], then you can decide to fix them and resubmit … or not.

You might need the help of a more grammatically inclined friend to spot and correct them all, but it might just be worth it if that's the ticket to publication.

YOUR FICTION VOICE

What I want you to see about all of these matters of grammar is that there may be a technical "error" involved in using them, but that's okay. Fiction is not the place for grammatical purity (unless you're writing a novel peopled entirely by characters who would be scrupulous about grammatical correctness).

If these things bother you personally, avoid misusing them. If not, don't give them a second thought.

Now, if your grammar problems extend beyond these gray areas into things like improper tenses or subject-verb agreement or other basic English skills, then I do recommend you get help with those. If you and yurn don't got no proper-like Englican skilz, you prolly got bigger misdemoners than you didn't even not know.

But on optional matters like the ones I've been covering here, you can pretty much do what you like. All I ask is that you *decide* to do them or not, instead of committing them without even realizing you're doing it. Blind spots are generally bad for novelists.

Fill in the blank: On the whole and for most novels I write, on these matters I will ____________. Though I reserve the right to change my mind for other projects, when it comes to gerunds, sentence fragments, passive voice, sentences that begin with conjunctions or participial phrases, and sentences that end with prepositions, I'm currently the sort of novelist who ________
____
____.

Chapter 16
BREAKING THE FOURTH WALL

Right now, in this sentence, I'm speaking directly to you, dear reader. Such things are done all the time in nonfiction. It's a conversation between author and reader, as if the two of us were sitting together having coffee (or, in my case, Mountain Dew).

But when it comes to fiction, some people say that such direct address should not be used. It's called breaking the fourth wall.

The fourth wall is a reference to the world of theatre, in which there may be three walls—the back wall upstage, left and right walls on either side of the stage—and then an open "wall" through which the audience watches the play. We subscribe to the illusion of that fourth wall, that the characters are unaware of the audience, and that all of this is really happening.

But occasionally, a character will acknowledge the presence of the audience and speak directly to them, thus breaking the fourth wall. It can be a jarring experience for the audience as that hermetically sealed membrane between fiction and reality is ruptured. This happens in movies, too, when a character speaks directly into the camera.

In fiction writing, you can find an example of breaking the fourth wall in the novel *A Star Curiously Singing* by Kerry Nietz. The narrator utters some science fiction jargon, and then we get this line: "That will take some explanation, I know. Don't worry, freehead, we'll get to that."

Let's explore the rule that thou shalt not break the fourth wall.

THOSE OPPOSED

Those who disagree with this rule point out that speaking directly to the reader is a rarely used technique in contemporary fiction, and that's part of what gives it its power. In fiction, as in theatre or cinema, being included in the characters' awareness can be disconcerting but effective.

I see it used when the novel comes in the form of a journal or retelling of events. So it's not that the characters pretend that the reader doesn't exist. It's more that the reader simply wasn't there at the time the events happened, but she *is* in the same time stream, maybe reading the journal long afterward or hearing the story from a "Call me Ishmael" narrator who speaks directly to her.

Breaking the fourth wall—or, better said, including the reader in the story—can be an effective way to shake things up and further engage the reader in the world of events being recounted.

THOSE IN FAVOR

Those who advise against breaking the fourth wall believe it's inherently a fiction error.

Breaking the fourth wall reminds them that they're reading a book and not watching the events unfold in real time. There is an existential jolt, and the element of covert observation—some would say *voyeurism*—is stripped away. You're caught. Noticed. Outed.

Whether they realize it or not, people who oppose breaking the fourth wall are believers in the invisible novelist philosophy of fiction. They want the mechanism of the storytelling to disappear, leaving the reader to notice only the characters and events.

According to that philosophy, "good" is anything that pulls the reader more deeply into the illusion that this is really happening, and "bad" is anything that knocks the reader out of that illusion.

MY OPINION

Breaking the fourth wall is a useful tool in the novelist's kit, but it should be done intentionally, as it really does have an impact on the reader—and it might push the reader out of the fictive dream. On the other hand, as with the "freehead" or "Call me Ishmael" examples, direct address might pull the reader more deeply into the world of the story, because now the characters are looking right at the reader.

I don't think it's something that should be done in every novel, and it will always remain experimental. That is as it should be, because it does change the reader-author contract. But if you have the sense that roping the reader into the story in this way will give your book an element you're looking for, why not give it a try? You can always take it out later if you don't like it.

TIPS FOR GETTING PAST THE GATEKEEPERS

Some agents and editors are not going to get it if you break the fourth wall in your fiction. Many will see it as an error and say you're not ready for prime time.

In that case, you have to choose carefully. Is the direct address something dear to you about this book, essential to its character? If so, leave it in and take your chances. If it's something you're not sure about, or if it's just kind of a throwaway thing you added, maybe take it out—or at least take it out of the first fifty pages. You can work with your editor to possibly put it back in later.

YOUR FICTION VOICE

Do you want to break the fourth wall? Is it something you enjoy in the fiction you read? Did you encounter a novel that did this and it appealed to you? If so, why not try it in yours? Or at least put it into your toolkit for possible use in the future. If you have encountered a book that did this and you hated what it did to you, then by all means leave it out of the fiction you write.

But if you do end up rejecting it for your own fiction, I hope you will refrain from telling other writers, especially unpublished ones, that breaking the fourth wall is a no-no in fiction. It isn't. It's a preference.

Fill in the blank: On the whole and for most novels I write, I _____________ break the fourth wall. Though I reserve the right to change my mind for other projects, when it comes to speaking directly to the reader, I'm currently the sort of novelist who _____ ____ ____.

Chapter 17
WEASEL WORDS

Originally, the term *weasel words* meant words or claims that, upon analysis, turn out to be empty. It can also refer to the attempt to imply meaning beyond the claim actually being made. It's equivocation and exaggeration. For example, if only *one* scientific study showed X, the weasel words version of it would be to say, "Studies have shown X."

But the term has now been brought into the world of fiction writing and, as you might guess, a rule has been born.

For fiction, weasel words are … well, any words the rulemaker feels don't belong in a novel. Here's one list I found:

- decided
- felt
- heard
- saw
- wanted
- knew
- could
- realized
- thought
- appeared
- noticed
- seemed
- looked
- understood

- considered
- believed
- supposed
- watched
- touched
- wondered
- recognized
- smelled
- wished

Another list I found added these, which are mostly equivocating words or phrases (and lots of *-ly* adverbs):

- a bit
- a little
- absolutely
- actually
- basically
- completely
- extremely
- just
- kind of
- mostly
- naturally
- often
- ordinarily
- particularly
- perfectly
- probably
- quite
- rather
- really
- so
- some
- somehow

- somewhat
- too
- totally
- truly
- usually
- very

Let's explore the "rule" that you can use so-called weasel words as much as you please.

THOSE OPPOSED

Weasel words sneak into your book and weaken the force of your prose. So instead of saying, "He was upset," you might say, "He was a bit upset."

These words tend to come in packs—hordes of weasels. Alone, each one doesn't weaken your book that much. But use them enough, or use enough of them, and your novel is riddled with little pockets of weakness that can—in the mind of the reader, at least—cause the whole thing to come crashing down.

THOSE IN FAVOR

Probably no one intentionally weakens his novel. If the author thinks the word is weak or doesn't carry the load he needs it to carry, he's not going to use it.

The idea that certain words are inherently weak—like *somewhat*—is absurd. To write an entire novel while having to avoid whole lists of words would be maddening and quite possibly (he said, using two weasel words at once) paralyzing. Even if you work on chasing out the weasels during the editing phase only, it's a silly exercise.

However, if you personally want to create a list of words that you would like to eliminate from your own writing, then by all means do so. This becomes your own kennel of pet weasels. That's great and reasonable and specific to you. Just don't try to impose that list on other writers.

MY OPINION

I don't worry about lists that someone has made telling me what words I can and can't use. A novel does not succeed or fail based on the presence or absence of certain words.

Now, if I'm editing a key passage and I'm just not feeling the power the way I want, I strengthen the words and sentence constructions I've used. If I end up replacing a word that someone has called a weasel word with something else, great. But I'm just as likely to replace someone's non-weasel word with what that person would call a weasel word—or two or three—and I don't let it bother me.

You can't write in fear of using some word that, like a lit stick of dynamite, will make your novel blow up. Realistically, your *characters* will use pretty much all the words on all the lists. Are you going to correct them? Just write and don't worry about it.

TIPS FOR GETTING PAST THE GATEKEEPERS

It's useless to try to predict what an agent or editor might consider a weasel word, or even if that person thinks in such terms at all. Worse, you might avoid every single weasel word on every list you can find on the Internet and yet end up with prose so wooden you could build a doghouse with it. Yay, you won the weasel prize but lost the publishing opportunity.

Didn't I once hear that writing fiction was supposed to be fun? I thought I heard that somewhere. Hmm.

YOUR FICTION VOICE

Do you have certain words you think are weak or annoying? Probably every writer does, whether she realizes it or not. If so, embrace your list and avoid those weasels as if they carried disease.

But if you're adopting someone else's list, and if those words never bothered you before, maybe chuck that list into the garbage can of silly rules and go on your merry way.

Whichever you choose, I hope you'll refrain from imposing your list on anyone else. One man's weasel word is another man's wonder word. (Yeah, I made that up. Didn't really work, but let's go with it.)

Fill in the blank: On the whole and for most novels I write, I ____________ weasel words. Though I reserve the right to change my mind for other projects, when it comes to what some people call weasel words, I'm currently the sort of novelist who _________
____
____.

Chapter 18
READ EVERYTHING

William Faulkner said, "Read, read, read. Read everything—trash, classics, good and bad, and see how they do it. Just like a carpenter who works as an apprentice and studies the master. Read! You'll absorb it. Then write. If it is good, you'll find out. If it's not, throw it out the window." Stephen King is a modern writer who gives the same advice.

Many teachers of fiction have taken Faulkner and King to heart and proclaim to all aspiring writers that they must always be reading fiction if they want to be taken seriously as a novelist.

Let's examine it, shall we?

THOSE OPPOSED

No one in publishing believes that aspiring novelists should ignore all fiction that has ever come before or is being produced now. You wouldn't even know you wanted to be a novelist if you hadn't encountered novels as a reader.

What some people object to is the idea that you have to "read everything" in fiction and be constantly reading more novels to make it as a novelist.

Many of these writers do enjoy reading fiction, but after a certain point—or perhaps while they're writing their own novels—they don't like to read other fiction. Maybe they don't want to be influenced by another writer when they're writing their own work. Maybe they don't want to be discouraged by reading someone whose skills seem to exceed their own. Maybe they are currently spending their novel-reading time doing research reading for their WIP (work in progress). Sometimes a writer can get so fed up with the fiction she sees around her that she doesn't want to put any more of it in her head.

And some novelists just don't like to read fiction that much. Of course they love story, but they enjoy *all* forms of story. Saying that all novelists must read all the fiction they can sounds suspiciously like someone's preference being turned into a rule.

THOSE IN FAVOR

Asking a novelist to read fiction shouldn't be unusual. You would expect a Hollywood director to enjoy watching movies, right? You would not be surprised to catch a basketball player watching some roundball on television. So of course a novelist ought to be reading novels. How else can he see what's out there, what's being done, what works and what doesn't, and what trends are developing? Agents and editors sometimes complain that new novelists haven't read enough in their chosen genre to be sure they're writing anything original.

When you read great fiction, you become inspired. You pick up techniques for your own writing. All over again, you come to appreciate the power a story can have.

When you read terrible fiction, you reinforce for yourself the things you want to be sure not to do. You see the techniques being done extremely poorly, and this acts as a cautionary tale for your own fiction.

When you read classic works of literature, you identify styles that are no longer in use—and some that might make a comeback—and you begin to glimpse the universal themes that can stand the test of time, themes you might find a place for in your own writing.

If you do want to be a better writer of fiction, you have to study other writers of fiction.

MY OPINION

I don't read much fiction. Isn't that funny?

Well, I actually read a ton of fiction in my role as freelance editor. I'm reading fiction all the time. And when I was running my own publishing house, which specialized in science fiction and fantasy (SF/F), I was reading it even more.

When I have time for leisure activities, a novel is not the first thing I think of to relax with. It feels too much like work. That's not to say that I'm ruined for novels, as I have favorites and I'm always curious about new SF/F novels or authors that people are raving about. I won't read them all, but I'll eventually get to some of them. Probably. As I write this, I'm reading a SF from a very small indie press, and I'm enjoying it quite a bit. But I'm more likely to pick up my PlayStation controller than I am a novel.

To infer that I can't grow as a novelist without reading other novels is ludicrous. I improve as a novelist by writing fiction. I improve by reading fiction craft books or learning from fiction teachers I respect.

But like any artist, I improve most as a novelist by enriching my life. I read nonfiction books on a variety of topics that interest me. I watch movies. I journal introspectively. I pursue spiritual goals. I take walks among the trees. I play with my kids. Out of that amalgam of input and output comes great fiction. That's true for the novelist who loves reading everything and for the novelist who would rather not.

TIPS FOR GETTING PAST THE GATEKEEPERS

This is a nonissue for gatekeepers. They won't be able to look at your fiction and go, "Oh, well, *this* is the work of someone who doesn't read enough fiction," or "Now *here's* the work of someone who reads enough fiction." What they're looking for is great fiction, and if you give that to them, they won't care if you read five novels a week or five in five years.

YOUR FICTION VOICE

What's your preference? If you love reading tons of fiction, then do it—it will certainly help you as a novelist. If you don't feel like reading other people's fiction all the time, then don't—it won't hurt you as a novelist.

What matters isn't whether you read novels all the time or if you rarely read novels. What matters is that your mind has what it needs to feel inspired to write fiction at your best. You—better than some rulemaker—know how to make that happen. Don't heed the rule; just do what you need to do to produce great fiction.

Be the sort of novelist you feel like being. Don't be anyone else's image of what a novelist ought to be or do or look like. Deal?

Fill in the blank: On the whole, I ____________ read as much fiction as I can get my hands on. Though I reserve the right to change my mind for other projects, when it comes to the advice to "Read, read, read," I'm currently the sort of novelist who ________
____
____.

Chapter 19 ELMORE LEONARD'S RULES

In the previous chapter I quoted one of William Faulkner's rules for fiction. Let's now look at another famous novelist's ten rules for fiction.

What I'm hoping you'll see by this point is that even the rules of a novelist who is hugely famous and successful are not laws but merely personal opinions and preferences. If you agree with them, fine. If not, don't sweat it. I hope that concept feels like a refreshing dip into a secluded lagoon every time you read it.

ELMORE LEONARD'S RULE #1

"Never open a book with weather."

Even if it really was a dark and stormy night, many say you shouldn't lead with that in your book—and you might avoid beginning your novel with a weather report simply because doing so has become a fiction cliché.

However, you might very much want to begin your novel with the weather. Sometimes a bolt of lightning might be nice, or a deluge, or the baking sun.

Just as beginning a novel with action might be a good idea or a bad idea, depending on how it's done, so beginning with weather is something you ought to be able to do in your book if it accomplishes your purpose.

ELMORE LEONARD'S RULE #2

"Avoid prologues."

We've already covered this topic at length. Use a prologue if you want to (but maybe call it chapter one).

ELMORE LEONARD'S RULE #3

"Never use a verb other than *said* to carry dialogue."

We've tackled this one, too. The use of the word *never* in a so-called rule of fiction ought to be the first indicator that it's someone's opinion being recast as a law.

I personally prefer *said* (and *asked*) as a speech attribution, but others feel differently, and that's okay. I myself will use the occasional *whispered* or *shouted,* which violates Leonard's rule.

ELMORE LEONARD'S RULE #4

"Never use an adverb to modify the verb *said*" (he admonished gravely).

We discussed this in a couple of previous chapters. If you want to stick with *said* while also avoiding *-ly* adverbs to modify it, go for it. But don't stress about it if you want to do it some other way.

Do you notice that if you were to obey this rule you'd be violating other rules that say you should use variety in your speech attributions? Whatever rule you adhere to, you're probably thereby violating someone else's rule. Don't get caught in that trap.

ELMORE LEONARD'S RULE #5

"Keep your exclamation points under control."

I happen to agree with this one. I think exclamation points in fiction should be constrained to dialogue and interior monologue. Using them in other places makes it look like the writer is nervous! Trying too hard to prop up weak prose by adding punctuation!!!

However, if an exclamation point comes to you—just flies out of your fingers—as you're writing a bit of prose, why not leave it in? The end user isn't going to mind one way or the other.

Gatekeepers might feel that exclamation points don't belong outside of character speech or thought. If so, maybe rein them in for the purposes of trying to get a contract. But after that, start sneaking them back in!

ELMORE LEONARD'S RULE #6

"Never use the words *suddenly* or *all hell broke loose*."

If something suddenly leaps into the character's awareness, it will happen *suddenly* whether you use that word or not. Sometimes, words meant to speed things along actually slow things down. Which of the following sentences reads faster?

> Immediately, without any warning whatsoever, purely by instinct and before he had a chance to react, working solely on adrenaline, Jim instantly ran to the door with all haste.
>
> Jim ran to the door.

Suddenly is a word that ends up making something feel *less* sudden.

Same with *then*. "Jim ran to the door. Then he opened it. Then he spoke to the person at the door. Then he let the person in. Then he shut the door."

If one thing is listed in a sequence *after* another thing, your reader will assume the first thing happened and *then* the next thing happened, without having to be told so with *then*.

As for "all hell broke loose," in addition to the above, it's a cliché.

However, what we're really getting here is Leonard's own set of weasel words. There's nothing illegal, immoral, or unethical about using these words. They're legitimate parts of the English language and therefore fair game for the novelist to use.

Certainly in dialogue, some characters might well use these words. We shouldn't let anyone's set of rules prevent us from allowing characters to speak as they really would.

While it's a good idea to avoid cliché in fiction, that doesn't mean there's never a time when a cliché isn't the perfect choice.

ELMORE LEONARD'S RULE #7

"Use regional dialect, 'patois,' sparingly."

Take this passage, for example:

> It made me shiver. And I about made up my mind to pray, and see if I couldn't try to quit being the kind of a boy I was and be better. So I kneeled down. But the words wouldn't come. Why wouldn't they? It warn't no use to try and hide it from Him. Nor from ME, neither. I knowed very well why they wouldn't come. It was because my heart warn't right; it was because I warn't square; it was because I was playing double. I was letting ON to give up sin, but away inside of me I was holding on to the biggest one of all.

According to Leonard, this shouldn't happen in fiction very often. It insults the reader's intelligence, they say, and the odd spellings knock him out of the illusion that he's watching this happen and instead remind him that he's reading a book.

Yes, Mark Twain could write this, but others shouldn't try it. He wrote classics.

Some fiction experts prefer that you spell everything correctly but achieve the semblance of regional dialects through word order. "You are to be finding the book black upon this table round, no?"

However, word-order strangeness is already kicking the reader out of the fictive dream, so why should nonstandard spellings be off limits?

> Whachu say'n y'all wanna do wi' dit now dat dem be catched?
> Yay-uh, 'm a-t'inkin' we-um oughta jess run.

If that's how your characters speak, and if that's how you want it to sound in the reader's head, why not write it in a way that will achieve the desired effect? However, keep in mind that, with this sort of thing, which can be difficult to read, a little goes a long way. Remind us every now and then that this is how the character speaks, but maybe don't ask the reader to have to plow through it too much.

I'd say this rule is something you can use if you want and ditch if you don't. Some gatekeepers will hold to the no-patois rule and others won't. You have no way of knowing who you'll get, so you might as well write it the way you prefer.

ELMORE LEONARD'S RULE #8

"Avoid detailed descriptions of characters."

This is clearly preference, as we discussed in our chapter on description. Some readers like detailed descriptions of characters (me, for one), and some readers don't. Give yourself permission to write it the way you prefer to read it, and don't worry if that agrees or disagrees with the esteemed Mr. Leonard.

ELMORE LEONARD'S RULE #9

"Don't go into great detail describing places and things."

Ditto. Pure preference.

ELMORE LEONARD'S RULE #10

"Try to leave out the part that readers tend to skip."

Wow, I love this one. It's beautifully general. I hope by now you've realized that there are a variety of readers. What some readers tend to skip, other readers crave, and vice versa.

But yes, by all means, leave out the parts that *you as a reader* tend to skip. That won't please all readers or gatekeepers, but it will please the readers and gatekeepers who are like you when it comes to fiction preferences, and that's not a small number.

We'll skip the part where I give my opinion on these, since I gave it as we went along. We'll also skip the gatekeepers part. As we've seen, agents and editors will be all over the place with these. Most won't be 100 percent pro-Leonard or 100 percent con, so there's no predicting it. Just make your own choices, but be willing to consider making changes if a gatekeeper requests them.

Fill in the blank: On the whole and for most novels I write, I ____________ follow Elmore Leonard's set of fiction rules. Though I reserve the right to change my mind for other projects, when it comes to anyone's set of rules, including those by established novelists like Elmore Leonard, I'm currently the sort of novelist who ____
____
____.

Chapter 20
THE BIG ENCHILADA

In this long chapter, I'm going to zip through dozens of other fiction "rules" I've heard and collected over the years.

By now, I'm confident you'll be able to predict what I'm going to recommend about each one:

- Understand why the rule is there in the first place.
- Consider whether you want to try it in your fiction or not.
- Determine what your own preference is, and do it that way.
- Be willing to consider changing it if a gatekeeper says that's one of the things preventing you from getting published or represented.
- Be free.

I'll give my thoughts or opinion on each of these, but your preferences are what matter in the end. The end user, our dear reader, probably won't know or care one way or another.

I've divided this chapter into two sections: rules that merit discussion and rules that are too silly to justify with much discussion.

I could've left you with the first list only, but because these silly ones are being bandied around and do their bit in rendering novelists paralyzed, and in an effort to provide as complete a list as I'm able, I'm going to mention them, too. Maybe the rule you're being accused of breaking is on the second list, and seeing it there will help you give it the influence it deserves.

OTHER FICTION "RULES" THAT MERIT DISCUSSION

Don't use present tense.

Present tense is the expected tense in some genres, but it's permissible in all. As is past tense.

Your chapters must be X number of pages long.

Just looking at the variety of numbers given for X ought to tip you off that there is no consensus here. I personally like my chapters to be around fifteen pages long (in a double-spaced Word document), but that's my preference. I've seen novels that worked very well with one- to two-page chapters and novels that worked very well with thirty-plus-page chapters. Do what you want.

Know the conventions of your chosen genre, and always give readers what they expect from that genre.

While it's important to know your genre's usual formulae and components, and while I agree that most genre fiction readers are wanting *more like that,* I won't say you shouldn't ever shake things around or do a genre mash-up. If you mess with the traditional pattern of romance, you may pay the price for it when readers complain in their reviews, but it's still an option that's open to you. Maybe you'll redefine the rules for your genre.

Your novel must be X number of words long.

As with chapter length, the "correct" overall word count for your manuscript changes every time you ask someone new. Generally speaking, something isn't considered novel length until it's 60,000 words or longer (though some say 50,000 and others say 65,000+). On the higher end, some publishers won't consider a book that is a word over 100,000 words long. Others won't consider it unless it's *at least* 150,000 words long. Fantasy epics tend to go longer; fiction for teens tends to run shorter. But in my opinion, you ought to let it be the length it wants to be and deal with shortening or lengthening it later, if you have to.

You must give every major (and all featured minor) characters their own introductory scene or moment the first time they step onstage.

I personally like this one, but I wouldn't call it a rule. I like defining my major characters and giving readers the right first impression about each one—plus, I find character intros fun to write—but other writers don't do this, and many of those books become bestsellers, too, so who knows?

Don't allow major characters to have names that are too similar or even begin with the same letter.

Well, Tolkien did okay with Saruman and Sauron, but I will admit I got the two confused as I first read *The Lord of the Rings*. If you have Devon and Damion and Darron and Derrick, then yeah, you might want to break out the baby name dictionary for a few of them—unless you did it on purpose. I personally try to choose very different names, because I don't like confusing readers on anything or knocking them out of the fictional illusion.

Begin your novel with an opening scene that lasts at least twelve pages.

This is a preference of mine. I like to well and truly begin my novels, not do little stutter steps. I'm all about hooking the reader and keeping her on the hook; breaking the scene before that has happened gives the reader the chance to throw the hook and get away. But I've seen many novels, including lots of bestsellers, that have much shorter beginning scenes, and they seem to do fine.

Avoid cliché phrases.

I personally don't like using clichéd terms like "He spun on his heel," or "It was so quiet you could hear a pin drop." I look for fresh ways of conveying the same feeling—but not so fresh that it knocks the reader out of the moment. I don't mind *characters* using clichés if that's what they'd really say. But so many best-selling novels are riddled with cliché phrases that I can't build a case that my way is better.

You should (or should not) italicize a character's thoughts.

For years, the convention has been to italicize a character's direct thoughts: "Jim sat down. *Wow, I'm hungry.*" Years ago, when I was still an impressionable writer (and not the curmudgeon I am now), I heard someone give the "rule" that thoughts should not be italicized. "I'm so sick of novelists italicizing thoughts. I get it already! Duh!" Well, I didn't want to be one of those backward writers who italicized thoughts, so I quit doing it and I told everyone else to stop doing it, too. Now I see that it was just this pretentious person's preference (like the alliteration?), and I'm free to do it as I please.

I actually like not italicizing thoughts, but as an editor I see that it's often confusing to the reader if they're not. Do what you want, but be consistent. If you don't italicize, you may hear a gatekeeper or crit group Nazi complain about it. If so, you can decide then what to do about it, if anything.

Don't structure your sentences so that what you mean as a descriptor comes across as a disambiguator.

I don't like it when novelists write things such as "She reached out with her shaking hands," and "He gazed upon her with his blue eyes and ran a hand through his greying red hair." The author means to be saying that her hands were shaking and that he had blue eyes and greying red hair. But grammatically, it reads as if the author is differentiating her shaking hands from some other sets of hands she might have brought with her, and that he could've chosen to look at her with his green eyes and run a hand through his black hair but didn't.

This is just my pet peeve, so don't worry about it. I'll think about seeing a counselor. Who knows, maybe I'll walk on my uncertain legs to see a psychiatrist (leaving my steady legs in the car).

But you might just scan your manuscript and decide if you could stand to change a few of these.

Keep your paragraphs to seven lines or fewer in length.

Some fiction teachers feel that paragraphs that go very long—eight lines or longer—are off-putting for the reader. Such paragraphs look like unscalable cliff faces, and this sends a subtle message to the reader that this is a difficult, tiresome book to read, one that will give no rest for the eyes or the mind. Shorter paragraphs break up the "face" of the page, making it look more accessible. I ascribe to this theory, but many best-selling novelists quite obviously do not. So do as you please.

Don't introduce too many characters and names too quickly or too early in a novel.

If this is something that bothers you, too, then definitely don't inflict it on you reader. Fans of some genres, like fantasy or science fiction, expect and even *want* to be a bit overwhelmed by all the strangeness at the beginning of the book, so they can generally tolerate more names and weirdness than people who are not fans of those genres.

By the way, you have permission to use that explanation in the crit group setting if people who don't write or read in your genre feel that something you've done isn't to their taste. So long as people who *do* like that genre will enjoy it, you're good. Hopefully, the crit group will get the differences between genres and back off a bit on that point.

You must be in a critique group if you want to succeed as a novelist.

This has proven true for some successfully published novelists and false for others. I've never had a good experience with a crit group, so I'm not a big fan. But many of my friends love their groups and have been with them so long they're more like family than just fellow writers. Much depends on the dynamics of the critique group; if those are healthy, it might be a good experience for you. Try one if you want, but don't be discouraged if it doesn't work out.

You must use deep POV.

Deep POV is the term some people have invented to refer to a way of writing prose that is neither dialogue nor internal monologue. Most authors lapse into "generic narrator voice" when they're writing the part of a scene that is description or narration. When they write dialogue or interior monologue, they do so in the voice of the character, but when they're writing the other stuff, they just sound like themselves. That narrator voice is the same in scenes when Claudette is the viewpoint character and when Jose is the viewpoint character. It's generic.

Deep POV says that everything—*everything*—in the book should be through the eyes of whichever viewpoint character you're currently writing. It's the difference between describing an event as you see it and describing an event as Adolf Hitler would see it. To use a theatrical term, using deep POV is like staying in character even when you're offstage.

I personally love this technique and think it should be the norm, not some advanced thing that only a few people try. Maybe give it a whirl yourself and see if you like it.

Don't write agenda-driven fiction.

What one person thinks is *message* or *theme* is what someone else might call agenda-driven fiction that preaches at the reader. If your whole purpose in writing a novel is to lecture to someone and point your literary bony finger at ne'er-do-wells, I suspect your writing may be subpar anyway. Folks who just want to whack other folks upside the head with a novel don't tend to have a huge amount of patience for learning the craft of fiction.

Is that to say you shouldn't have a theme to your writing? Not at all. I'm writing what could be termed an agenda-driven book after becoming alarmed over a trend I was seeing. I'm still creating great characters and giving it great structure and doing everything else I know to make it good fiction, but I can't deny that there is a message I want to get across. Whether it will be too heavy-handed or not remains to be seen.

With your own fiction, don't shy away from the things you're passionate about, but be careful about wanting to use your book as a bludgeon.

Don't use buried dialogue.

Buried dialogue is when a character's spoken words are buried or hidden inside character action. For example:

> Belinda opened the door. "What are you doing here?" She crossed her arms, determined to show him she meant business. "I told you to stay away." Why was he there anyway? Didn't he know what was good for him?

The spoken words in this passage are buried, and some argue this slows the pace of the book and steals the oomph of the dialogue. This is purely someone's opinion.

Don't use flashbacks in the opening chapter.

This is one I agree with, but that doesn't make it any less of a preference or opinion. Novels with flashbacks in the opening chapter have sold well. And if the whole opening chapter is a flashback, it's not a flashback at all but a prologue, and you already know how I feel about prologues.

What I personally find awkward is the book that begins with one paragraph of setting, like, "Jane sat on her porch and looked across the cornfields," and then immediately goes into flashback. We're barely oriented in the scene and we're off into another one. Usually, we get more oriented in the flashback scene than in the scene it's supposedly flashing back from.

I'm not a fan of flashbacks at any time in a novel, though I acknowledge they can be used beautifully, as in the old TV series *Lost*, for example. But in fiction, my feeling is that they usually bore the reader and are a form of telling, which is sort of saying the same thing.

If you're wanting to strengthen how engaging your opening chapter is, and you find that you've included a flashback in that chapter, that's an item to consider removing. Let your reader get his bearings in your story before asking him to adjust to a previous scene.

Don't start a novel with a dream.

Yes, it is a cliché to start a novel (or a chapter) by putting the hero in some terrifying scenario and then just waking him up and revealing that it was only a dream. And yes, it's often a good idea to avoid cliché in fiction. But what if the novel is *about* dreams? What if it is, to quote *The Princess Bride,* a "dweam wiffin a dweam"? What if you're writing *The Matrix* and all of reality is a dream?

If I can think of that many exceptions off the cuff, maybe it's not such a hard and fast rule after all. If you want to start your novel with a dream, and you have a good reason for doing so (and you can handle the people telling you that you shouldn't have done it), go for it.

Don't use parentheses or semicolons in fiction.

I personally prefer my fiction sans parentheses or semicolons. The former feel too nonfictiony and the latter feel too grammarian. But if you love (or hate) these or other elements of punctuation in your fiction, then by all means go with your preferences. Some may tell you not to, but those are just *their* preferences showing.

You must not use more than one name per viewpoint character.

In other words, don't write, "Jim sat down on the janitor's couch and ate the former Navy SEAL's bean dip. The southpaw put his feet up on the Texan's coffee table and kicked Skippy's shoes off." So, how many people were in this scene? How many people were referred to? If you answer any number other than one, you're incorrect.

Referring to characters in multiple ways like this is confusing for the reader. However, it's also a sneaky form of telling, since we learned a lot about this fellow without having to discern it for ourselves. I'd endeavor to keep the reader oriented (if such is your goal), but beyond that, the sky's the limit.

Don't ask rhetorical questions in fiction.

Actually, this rule is often voiced for nonfiction, too, and as you've no doubt seen, I don't pay it much heed, do I?

But asking the reader a question, especially one that wants the reader to agree with your narrator, is a risk. If you write, "Corrie wasn't any good for me, was she?" and some smart-aleck reader—like me—says to himself, "Actually, I don't care, but if you got what you deserved, you'd get a full diet of Corrie three times a day forever!" Ahem. In that case, you may have just invited your reader to realize that she's not as connected to your story as she thought, and she might just put it down and give up.

That said, this isn't a rule or even a strong suggestion. It's a tool in your kit to either use or not, *n'est-ce pas*?

Don't dump backstory in the first chapter.

Well, if you're going to just dump it, I encourage you to avoid doing so in the beginning. Sacking the reader with pages of, "Ten years ago, Jake repaired submarines in his submarine shack in Florida. It was the happiest time in his life," blah, blah, blah, is not going to make your reader feel like sticking with your book.

But as for establishing information the reader needs to know for later, that certainly does belong in the first chapter. Should it be done in an information dump? Not according to my preferences. But showing us that Jake knows how to repair submarines because later he's going to need to do so to save the world ... yeah, that sort of "backstory" (rather, *information*) is appropriate for the first chapter.

The question is not in whether you convey information but in how you do it. How could you show that Jake knows how to repair submarines?

If the question is whether or not you should dump backstory, then my personal preference is that you shouldn't do it at all, and especially not at the beginning when the reader is still deciding if she wants to read this book or not. However, lots of best-selling novels do just this, so it obviously isn't always the death knell for reader engagement.

But if the question is whether or not you ought to be *conveying information* to the reader, including information about things in the past or things that gave rise to the current situation, then I think it should be fair game.

In *Mulan,* the prologue shows the villain bringing his army over the Great Wall of China. He tells the guard on the wall that, by building this wall, the Emperor had all but invited him to come invade. Now, isn't that backstory? Isn't that information about something that happened before the current scene?

The reason it isn't a backstory dump is that it came as an engaging part of a scene that was meeting all the criteria of a great opening. The story didn't come to a screeching halt in order to back the truck up and dump on the reader, in other words. Engaging story elements delivered in an engaging way, even if they're technically backstory, are welcome in any chapter, including the first.

Don't begin a scene with dialogue.

What's most important is to engage the reader. Many times, you can write a line of crackling dialogue that does a much better job of grabbing the reader's attention than a paragraph of scene-setting. I think you ought to be allowed to begin your scenes however you jolly well please.

Do not begin a scene with unattributed dialogue.

This is probably an attempt to get the reader oriented right away as to who is speaking. I like that goal, but I can conceive of scenarios in which delaying the revelation of the speaker's identity would be desirable.

Don't/always set your book in a real/fictitious town.

There are pros and cons to both. Set it in a real place, and real residents may love (or hate) the book because of it. Set it in a fictional place, and you won't run the risk of offending anyone in a real place but lose the possibility of real residents getting behind your book. Each is the right decision in a variety of situations. Do take your pick.

Don't/always use real/fictitious names of people.

Mostly the same answer, but using the names of real people can be tricky, especially if you're maligning a real person who isn't a public figure. Public figures are fair game (for the most part). It's a lot more effective to set a story in the White House administration of, say, Bill Clinton than to make up the administration of Jerry Wiggins. Or you could do a hybrid: Make up most of the names of the people in your book but refer to real humans by name to give a realistic flavor of the time. It's up to you.

You must answer the so what? *and* or else ... ? *questions.*

A writer friend reminded me that he and I met at a conference, and as he told me about his novel idea, I kept interrupting him with "So what?" I wasn't trying to irritate him (I hope!) but trying to get him to see that the reader needs to be concerned about your book's outcome or she may not want to keep reading.

So what? probably has more to do with reader engagement in the hero, whereas the *or else … ?* question is about stakes. If the hero doesn't do X, what will be the result, not only to the main character but to everyone else in the story? Both are good questions to answer, and I regularly ask them of my editing clients. Play around with upping the stakes and reader engagement, and see if you like the results.

By the end of the book, all loose ends must be tied off.

The average reader does enjoy closure at the end of the book, but I can think of several scenarios in which you might want to leave some questions unanswered and some *t*s uncrossed. Just do it intentionally, not because it simply didn't occur to you to let the reader know if Susie ever did get her scholarship or what happened to the puppy after the big wreck at the climax.

You must have a strong female protagonist.

This is an example of trend-chasing, which I despise, so I might portray a weak female protagonist just to thumb my nose at what someone says I *have* to do. If the story in your mind calls for a strong female hero, write one. If not, don't. If you are told by a gatekeeper to add one, maybe do it (and maybe don't). Make this decision based on what's right for your story, not what you fear will happen if you don't write it a certain way.

Do not include unimportant dialogue.

This is an effort to make every word and sentence advance your plot, reveal character, or develop relationships. If you write dialogue that does none of those things—that simply goes off on a tangent, is really just you on your soapbox, or is otherwise extraneous—consider cutting it. But maybe you feel the line gives the right flavor or nudge to the moment or character. It's your book, right?

You must vary your sentence structure and length.

I like this one. Having the same rhythm of sentence too often can become repetitive. Whenever I catch myself repeating a sentence structure, I work to vary it. But I don't worry too much about it. You probably shouldn't, either. Tools, not rules.

You must introduce the main character in the opening chapter.

Not if you use a prologue that features other characters. And not if your story is one in which the main character isn't even around, like a murder mystery,.

The movie *Jaws* began with minor characters, one of whom gets eaten. The main character didn't show up until later, and that story seemed to do pretty well.

You must have a mentor character.

This is probably a sidelong reference to the hero's journey (Joseph Campbell's monomyth) and/or Carl Jung's theory of archetypes. The Mentor (usually capitalized) is like Merlin, Gandalf, or Obi-Wan Kenobi—a wise older man who guides the hero into maturity but then is no longer available to the hero when his true test comes. It's a useful and powerful tool, but feel free to use it or not.

Avoid the mirror trick.

Ah, the mirror trick, in which a character happens to pass in front of a mirror and catch her reflection, thus triggering a full description of what she looks like, including her flashing emerald eyes and flowing brown locks. This is a great example of a new problem that arises when writers are trying to avoid breaking some other rule of fiction. To stick with a disciplined POV, the viewpoint character can never describe herself. I mean, why would she? She already knows what she looks like, and it's hard to find a reason for why she would suddenly do so. So the mirror trick was born: She can stay inside her own head and yet still describe herself.

In my opinion, the reader won't know or care if you just outright explain (yes, in telling and in a POV violation) what she looks like. As for the mirror trick, it's a cliché only in the minds of agents and editors—most readers don't care, and they're grateful to know what the person looks like, however that comes about.

A great way to skirt the issue, in my opinion, is to have the viewpoint character look in the mirror but give a *skewed and inaccurate* description of what he looks like: "Meh, hair not as matted as usual and not so dirty that it looks like mud; eyes not as red as last night." That retains proper POV and *sort of* gives a description, but it's incomplete. Use other characters describing the character—"Hey, gorgeous, where's a blonde like you been all my life?" to fill in the rest.

You must use a three-act structure.

I have occasionally heard novelists complain that they don't want to use three-act structure because it's a formula or it's limiting or something. Ostensibly, they want to be free to create a story that is entirely fresh.

Hmm, well, I applaud the impulse, but I doubt the feasibility of the plan. Three-act structure isn't a formula so much as an *observation* of the shape all stories have.

Consider someone giving a speech before a crowd. As soon as he gets up to speak, he makes some opening remarks to prepare the audience for what is to come. Then there is the body of the speech. And then there are some concluding remarks at the end.

That is three-act structure. You can try to write a novel that defies that structure, but my guess is that you're going to end up following it, all the same. Won't you need to begin it in a way that prepares the reader for what is to come? Don't you then have the main story? Isn't it all finished by tying things off?

Now, you could certainly provide the middle section only, giving the reader the experience of finding random chapters pulled from a larger book. It would give an experimental feel that might work for a book here or there. But if you want your novel to be taken seriously by publishers and readers, your story will need setup and introductions (act one), the heart of the tale (act two), and a way to bring it all to a head and then tie it off (act three).

Three-act structure is no restriction. It is an organizational scheme that ensures your novel has all the elements it needs to make the story feel complete.

Don't use the deus ex machina *device.*

That's the ancient theatrical practice of ending a play by having a god appear and sort everything out: "You marry her, you go to jail, and you become king." In modern fiction, the *deus ex machina* manifests as a sudden stroke of luck or some implausible event that saves the day. I like the adage "Don't let good luck or the Good Lord save your hero." In my opinion, it's better to have the characters figure things out for themselves.

However, I can imagine a story in which good luck or the Good Lord do save your hero—especially if the book is about one or both of those things. Hey, if a *deus ex machina* works for your story, give it a shot. Gatekeepers may object, but the end reader may not care or even notice.

Don't allow characters to serve plot.

By "character serving plot," I mean moments in which characters do things they would never do in order to allow the plot to proceed as the writer prefers.

My favorite example of this is in Michael Crichton's *The Lost World*. A scientist who is a radical purist about not tainting the environment the dinosaurs live in later unpeels a candy bar and tosses the wrapper to the ground. Obviously, this is something that character would never do. But the author, rest his soul, needed the dinosaurs to have a way to connect this character with the idea of candy—so they would eat him. Thus the candy wrapper.

My own preference is to never force characters to serve plot, but stories that do force characters to serve plot are sometimes quite popular, as the previous example illustrates. But I also understand the need for certain things to happen in the plot, and it is your story, in the end. I would urge you to find a way to have everything happen that you want to happen, but in ways that allow your characters to remain true to who they are.

Don't edit as you go; wait until the rough draft is finished.

This feels like one writer's personal style that has been extrapolated out to become a rule for all writers. When and how a writer edits is something every writer should decide for herself.

I understand the idea of keeping the writer's hat on and not allowing the critic's hat to come out until the story is on paper. It's possible to become paralyzed by trying to make the first page (or scene or chapter) "perfect" before moving on. But I personally like to read and touch up the last couple of pages I wrote during my previous writing session as a way to get back into the headspace of the story and ramp up to writing new material the next day.

Just find your own way here, and don't let someone else's preference become a rule for you.

Write only what you know.

This is great for some writers and not so great for others. I personally don't write what I know but what I'm curious about. I go learn it first and *then* write about it, so I guess I am abiding by this rule, in a way.

You probably don't want to write on topics about which you have absolutely no clue, as you may come off sounding ridiculous. But I don't agree with constraining yourself to writing about things you already know inside and out.

Avoid stereotypical characters.

There are pros and cons on this one. The advantage to stereotypes is that they're instantly recognizable and understood in our culture. Of course, they are oversimplifications and can end up as offensive, sexist, and/or racist, but something doesn't become a stereotype unless it is seen so often in reality as to become recognizable at a glance.

The disadvantage to stereotypes is that they're unrealistic and shallow. Even if someone *is* a proper Brit, it doesn't mean he's smart or a supervillain. You might actually find a Mexican named José, but that doesn't mean you know all about him already. As for dumb blondes, how is that the sum total of a living human feature? If your novel is peopled with stereotypes, you may lose the many readers who desire realistic characters in the fiction they read.

It's possible to play against type, however, and that can be fun. Like you bring on a redneck from the sticks, but he's actually a neuroscientist. You bring on the shrew, but you reveal that she's behaving in those ways only to protect someone else.

On the whole, I prefer that you work harder on your characters rather than just trot out a type. But sometimes, the type is exactly what you need.

In my painting, most of the time I'm after a look that is fresh and arresting. But I also create the occasional political cartoon, which must be instantly readable in one frame. In that case, the more stereotypical you can be, the better. But when you're aspiring to art—in painting or in fiction—most of the time you will want to avoid stereotype.

Don't let the protagonist be a fictional version of yourself (the writer).

I see the logic in this, especially if you are, like me, a plot-first novelist for whom realistic characters do not come easily. Making the hero like you can lead to an even more unrealistic character, as real people act in inconsistent ways, and yet we expect fictional characters to have a consistent core from scene to scene.

However, the typical author has no one else to draw on besides himself when he's writing a variety of characters in a variety of situations. How will the hero deal with something the writer has never experienced? The writer will have to draw from similar situations he's been in and do some extrapolating.

The point is that we're always basing our characters on ourselves, even if we don't mean to. You might want to consciously choose major aspects of your hero that are different from your own personality. But then again, you might not.

You must have a likeable protagonist.

I personally agree with this one, but you can write a successful novel with an unlikeable protagonist. We want our hero to go through a transformation during the story, so she has to begin "low" so she can come to soar with eagles. But even in those cases, I like to give a glimpse of what's likeable about her so the reader doesn't mind hanging with her for a few hundred pages. Nobody wants to be stuck with a jerk on a very long car trip. Still, some movies have unlikeable protagonists, and they can work. Perhaps it will work for you in your novel.

You must have dialogue on your first or at least second page.

The argument here is that dialogue is interesting and other stuff is not, so if you don't have dialogue on those opening pages, you'll never engage your reader. This is pure preference. Reader engagement is always our goal, but dialogue is not the only way to achieve it.

Don't let your villain be completely evil.

I agree that a purely evil villain is not as nuanced or realistic as one with a mixture of good and evil, but so what? Some stories work better with a villain who can be safely determined as The Bad Guy.

Avoid split infinitives.

Here's an infinitive: "to go." Here's a split infinitive: "to boldly go" (where no one has gone before). Obeying every dictate and recommendation of the grammarian crowd won't win you many readers, so don't stress about split infinitives or any of the similar dictates we've examined.

Avoid ten-dollar words.

This depends on your philosophy of fiction. If you're of the invisible novelist school, you'll probably agree with this one. If you're of the painted paragraphs school, you'll find those ten-dollar words worth every penny you paid for them. This is your preference.

Don't overuse ellipses, especially in your characters' dialogue.

I happen to like ellipses (and em dashes), but I try not to use too many of them on the given page. It can begin to look amateurish. Really, anything you do (in fiction) over and over without realizing it may be a blind spot for you. I'd prefer you use ellipses because you want to and not because it's a habit you're not aware you have.

Kill your darlings.

When it comes to fiction, this phrase means you should find your pet phrases and favorite elements and reduce the number of times you use them. Things in your blind spot may be glaring to your reader, so I think this is a good idea.

Figure out the worst thing that could happen to your hero, and then do that to him.

This feels like a fun workshop activity for writers conferences or critique groups, but it's not a rule. It might be a useful tool, though.

Never discuss theme in your opening pages.

If you're going to have an actual discussion of, say, man's inhumanity to man, the first chapter isn't the place for it. You're all about engaging the reader in those chapters, after all, and a philosophical discussion about anything is not as likely to do that as action and dialogue might be.

But if you had a more interesting scene that *pertained* to the theme, then you're onto something.

SILLY FICTION "RULES" THAT DON'T MERIT DISCUSSION

Believe it or not, all of the following have in fact been used to "correct" novelists. I hope you'll see that they're pure preference. If you agree with any of them, feel free to use it in your writing. Just please don't try to force it on other writers.

I hope you'll excuse my not exactly reverent tone as I respond to these. It gets to me when people in positions of authority (even in the critique group setting) impose ridiculous restrictions on writers who don't yet have enough experience to know that they don't deserve attention.

Don't use any dialogue tags (a.k.a., speech attributions).

Seriously? None? I guess they're all supposed to be changed to beats? I can see the Amazon reviews now: "I gave this novel 5 stars because it had no dialogue tags. The story and characters were junk, but it was just such a joy to read a novel without tags that I felt compelled to …"

Crack down on every rule violation you see in another writer's fiction.

Ah, the crit group Nazi's call to arms. I'd like you to consider a kinder, gentler approach to the comments you make on someone's fiction. Instead of saying, "No," why not say, "What if … ?" And instead of saying, "What if," why not say, "I personally think this is working just fine, and it's clearly a matter of opinion and preference, but some gatekeepers may ding you for doing X"?

Don't write in first person.

Hmm, I guess this one is designed to reflect (or chase? or avoid?) a trend. If you like fiction written in first person, use it in your own fiction. You may hear a gatekeeper say that's so last year or whatever, so at that point you can change it if you want to.

The thing about trends is that sometimes they come around again later. Most of the time, a *trend* is simply whatever is hot right now. So if you write something, in whatever way you feel like writing it, and it becomes popular, suddenly you're a trendsetter!

Or perhaps this "rule" is designed to tell writers not to use first person because it's a POV style that is allegedly harder to write in than third person. That may be, but it should still not be given as a rule. If the writer wants to try his hand at first person, why not let him?

Don't use teenagers as characters.

Do I even need to comment?

You must (or must not) use—or at least "properly" spell—words like alright/all right *or* okay/OK, *and* towards/toward.

Aw, don't sweat this stuff. If you have a preference, use it. If not, at least strive for consistency.

Keep your cast of characters traditional (e.g., hero, love interest, villain, mentor, etc.).

More hero's journey/archetype preferences. Tools, not rules.

Don't use stage direction (like "The following day ..." or "He went to the window ...").

Just silly, in my opinion. Use stage direction if you like it. I do.

Don't use complete sentences in dialogue.

Okay, I understand that this is an attempt to achieve verisimilitude in dialogue—since often we don't speak in complete sentences in reality. But I can't see this working for a whole novel.

My preference would be to write dialogue using complete sentences sometimes and incomplete sentences other times. I actually do finish my spoken sentences sometimes in the real world. This shouldn't be a rule that shackles writers but rather a suggestion for a way to vary dialogue and approach verisimilitude.

Don't use the word could, *as in, "She could see him."*

The word *could* drives some writers crazy, though I'm not exactly sure why. Perhaps it is a case of something that could (ahem) be replaced by something "stronger." Like instead of "She could see him," it could be "She saw him." Maybe it's on someone's weasel word list.

This is perhaps another item for the category of what might be done to strengthen a key passage but might also be left alone.

Always/never use beta readers.

Using test readers to comment on your book before you consider it finished can be a good idea. At their best, they can spot things a professional editor would see and help you drastically improve your manuscript (for free!). At their worst, they can make you want to pluck your eyes out and never try to write again. So … do what you want.

You should write all your paragraphs in this order: action, emotion, dialogue.

Seriously?

You should introduce your protagonist by first and last name, never first name alone.

These are just getting silly.

You must place only *and* just *where they belong.*

A writer friend of mine designed a T-shirt to promote her fantasy novels. She wrote something that most folks would've phrased like this "Be silent, look wise, and only eat those who annoy you." But, being a writer, my friend was more careful about her placement of *only,* so she wrote it as, "Be silent, look wise, and eat only those who annoy you."

To be grammatically correct, you should place words like *only* and *just* right before the words they modify. The former phrasing above puts the limiter on *eat,* which isn't where the writer meant it. As if he should only eat the person, not also drink the person, murder the person, teach the person, etc. The limiter is put on the wrong thing, in other words. But how many of us—writers included—say it this way all the time in speech, and people know what we mean without any problem?

Some characters will certainly say it incorrectly, and if you're using so-called deep POV, even descriptions and narration will be in the character's voice, which means it will be wrong there, too. It should be made grammatically correct *only* if you're endeavoring to be perfect in your English in your narration and/or when certain characters who would get it right are doing the speaking.

Don't start every paragraph with a character name.

I can see how this would be repetitive and how varying things would be a good idea, but the end reader won't notice or mind either way.

This also goes for the rule to not start multiple paragraphs with the same word, even if it's not a name. Variety is nice for the eye, but it hardly rises to the level of rule, in my opinion.

Don't let dialogue go longer than three lines.

Someone's arbitrary rule, it seems to me. It's often a good idea, in my opinion, to break up dialogue and include beats or stage business to lock us into the moment and keep it from becoming a talking heads affair, but if a long passage of dialogue works for certain spots in your book, why not go for it?

Don't overuse the words look *or* looked.

I had an editor tell me one time that I overused the word *look,* as in "It looked like she would be late," or "He looked over at her." It was invisible to me, so I (sort of) appreciated having it pointed out to me. But now I don't worry about it. If you want to *look* for and reduce repetition of this word or any other, you should do so. Maybe you'll find something you didn't know you were doing, and that's always a win.

Always use words with Anglo-Saxon roots over words with Latin roots.

So you'd use *saw* instead of *perceived* and *gave* rather than *donated.*

Huh. That's all I have to say about that one.

Don't start paragraphs with the word I.

Apparently, having a number of paragraphs that begin with this pronoun puts all the focus on the speaker, who is obviously very self-centered. I generally agree with the idea of including a variety of sentence and paragraph structures, but I doubt a book will stand or fall based on something like this.

Never have more than three POV characters in a novel.

Apparently this rule was given in an effort to limit the viewpoint characters so as to channel the reader's affections to a finite number of outlets.

I applaud the impulse here, but I've seen highly successful novels that fully engage their readers despite a large number of viewpoint characters. Thrillers, especially—like those by Tom Clancy—do this and thrive.

Do what you feel is right for your novel, and don't worry about the number of POV characters.

Your protagonist must always fail until the climax of the book.

Wow. Strange. I guess this is designed to make the reader think the hero will fail in the climax, which will supposedly increase suspense as the climax approaches. Maybe these folks feel that allowing the hero to succeed at anything will cause reader engagement to die because now it seems like the hero will be okay.

Not sure, but I personally don't think you need to deprive your poor hero of every success. Maybe it would work at a certain juncture in a particular book, but I can't see it working as a rule. I'm not sure I could keep reading a novel in which the hero is no good at anything.

Never write across gender lines.

So, if you're a female writer, you should never write a male protagonist, and vice versa.

Hmm. Well, I suspect it would be more difficult for the typical male writer to write a believable female protagonist, but that doesn't mean none of us should try.

As for female novelists writing male protagonists, that might be easier to pull off. I once commented on how well novelist T. L. Higley wrote male characters, and she said, "Jeff, you guys aren't that hard to understand." I'll leave you to fill in the blanks on that one.

Never use QNID—questions not in dialogue.

We'll end with one I heard about at a writers conference. It's a rule that must certainly be true because it has an acronym! QNID: question not in dialogue. Ah, the power of an official-sounding acronym. Seriously, who makes up these things?

An example of a QNID is when the viewpoint character asks a silent question in reaction to something. So maybe the character sees someone she wasn't expecting, and then the writer writes: What's he doing here?

Okay, according to the QNID police, that is verboten. Because it's a question, but it's not in dialogue (or in italics, I guess), which means it violates the QNID dictum and must therefore be struck from the manuscript.

Sigh. Even if a rule has a slick acronym, it doesn't mean it's any more binding than anything else we've looked at in this book so far. I personally see no reason not to—and several reasons *to*—include a QNID. So write them to your heart's desire (or … TYHD).

TO SUMMARIZE

Robert McKee begins his book *Story* with these words:

> Story is about principles, not rules. A rule says, "You must do it this way." A principle says, "This works … and has through all remembered time." The difference is crucial. … Anxious, inexperienced writers obey rules. Rebellious, unschooled writers break rules. Artists master the form.

Chances are, you've been an anxious, inexperienced writer eager to learn and obey all the rules. I have. Nearly every novelist goes through that phase. If that's where you are now, then feel free to make liberal use of the rules and methods that help you write your book. If they help you, how can that be anything but good?

But eventually you'll reach the point where the rules become a hindrance to you. You'll still agree with some of them, but you'll see that most of them are dependent upon situation and may vary from project to project. You'll also see other writers avoiding the rules and ending up with successful novels. Hopefully, that will result in you finding your own set of preferences as well.

Professional copy editors can worry about gerunds, "to be" verbs, and split infinitives. The rest of us, most especially the vast majority of readers, don't care about them. The joy of fiction is the ability to use (and abuse and play with) English, not be defeated by the formals of precise grammaticism.

It is inevitable that you will encounter people who will say you'll never get published if you do (or don't do) X, Y, and Z. Depending on where you are in your confidence level as a writer, such admonitions might seem authoritative to you, especially if the person imposing the rule is a gatekeeper.

I hope you understand these people are merely giving their preferences, their opinions, and their own personal brand of paralysis. If they were told not to do something, then you must be told as well. No fair that you get away with it if they don't.

If you respect the person giving you the rule, I have a two-step recommendation for you. First, be teachable. Try the new rule on for size, not as something you must do but as something new you're experimenting with. If you like it, use it—but don't try to impose it on anyone else. If you don't like it, don't think twice about ditching it. If the rulemaker is the leader of your crit group and she just won't let it die, maybe it's time to find (or form) a new crit group.

The second step is to stop being teachable. You can't keep throwing out your opening pages because first one person, then another, then some other group, then some teacher, and then some random person on the bus all keep telling you what to change. At some point you have to stop being so flexible and just decide how you want to write the thing. If you keep letting the "experts" cause you to doubt yourself, you'll end up in misery.

So, be teachable, try it on, then stop being teachable and find your own style.

We talked earlier about Elmore Leonard's famous rules of fiction. Years ago, my novelist friend Tom Morrissey taught on faculty at the same writers conference with Leonard. They exchanged signed novels, and for whatever reason, Leonard read Tom's book overnight.

At breakfast the next day, he said, "Hey, Tom. I read your book. This is pretty good shit." Tom pointed out to him that he was pretty sure that his novel had broken every single one of Leonard's ten rules of writing.

"Yeah," Leonard said, "but that's all right, because you did it like you knew what you were doing. And if you know what you're doing, the rules don't apply."

Part Two
THE GREAT COMMANDMENT OF FICTION

> "Your job as a writer is to have the reader become the characters."
>
> —Dr. Paul J. Zak, neuroscientist

I've spent the bulk of this book debunking the so-called rules of fiction. We've seen that they're not really rules, certainly not in the sense that the *Chicago Manual of Style* catalogues the list of rules for English grammar and usage. We've seen that these rules are really just preferences and opinions. At best, they're useful for the brand-new writer just wanting to know *one* way to write a book, and a few of them are good tools to try out if a certain section of your novel isn't working as you'd like.

Indeed, most of the time, these rules come into play only when something is going wrong. When the reader is utterly captivated by a story, the writer might be doing 101 things wrong (in terms of these rules, anyway), but because the reader is engaged, no one cares to question how or why it's working. It's when the reader is not captivated that we start pulling out the rules and trying to analyze what's going on.

The results of such an investigation can be helpful or disastrous. In my opinion, it's usually the latter, especially when well-meaning people begin saying that the novel isn't working because of the failure to apply these many (and contradictory) rules of fiction.

Theoretically, some of these rules can be used to strengthen a section (or an entire manuscript) that isn't working. Can a page of backstory be replaced with showing and thus improve that spot in the book? Absolutely. Can weak verbs be replaced with stronger verbs and thus punch up that paragraph? Certainly. Can a consistent POV keep the reader more oriented, and can the removal of gerunds subtly strengthen a passage, and can dialogue be improved by cutting down on the number of complete sentences used? Yes, yes, and yes.

But to say that the correct application of these rules are what *makes* a novel excellent is utterly fallacious. The avoidance of error is not the same as the achievement of art. Simply obeying all the rules, if it were even possible, wouldn't give you a good novel any more than obeying all traffic rules would make you a championship race car driver.

The secret to irresistible fiction isn't to properly use rules. The secret to irresistible fiction is to do whatever it takes to gain the reader's interest and hold it to the end of the book. If there was one rule I thought held true for every novelist, if I had to give one great commandment of fiction, it would be this:

You must engage your reader from beginning to end.

A good novel is one you love reading—and that you do actually continue reading—to its completion. That's my definition, which is pretty much where we were when we started this book.

My first goal was to remove the giant, paralyzing tumor that was resting against the spinal cord of your fiction writing.

My second goal is to show you how to flex your muscles in the only exercise that truly matters in fiction: engaging your readers and keeping them engaged.

For that, we will turn to the brain.

YOUR BRAIN ON FICTION

What's going on inside your brain when you get interested in a novel? What's going on in there when you're *not* interested in a novel?

If you could figure out what's happening in the brain when you read a good or bad novel, perhaps you could intentionally do the things in your writing that would cause others to love *your* novel and avoid the things that would cause readers to lose interest.

Brain hacking, in other words.

To find out if such a thing were possible, I contacted Dr. Paul J. Zak, founding director of the Center for Neuroeconomics Studies and Professor of Economics, Psychology and Management at Claremont Graduate University. Dr. Zak also serves as Professor of Neurology at Loma Linda University Medical Center. He is the author of *The Moral Molecule,* and you can learn more about him at www.pauljzak.com.

Dr. Zak does laboratory work studying the effects of story on the brain, so when I read an article by him on the subject, I knew I had to interview him.

Turns out, it is possible to use knowledge of how the brain works to gain and maintain reader interest. In fact, novelists and filmmakers have been doing it for generations, and storytellers of all kinds have been doing it for millennia. But what we've been stumbling upon in the dark, Dr. Zak's research allows us to do on purpose.

Part Two of this book explores how this is done. We'll look at what's going on in your brain when you encounter narrative, why it works when it works, why it doesn't when it doesn't, and how to tap into the power of brain chemistry to make sure readers engage with your novel and stay engaged to the end.

Chapter 21
HACKING YOUR READER'S BRAIN

First, a disclaimer. The brain is hugely complex, and scientists are only just beginning to understand how it works. What I've included in this section is a vast oversimplification of what's going on up there. Your reader's brain is attending to 1,001 other things besides reading your novel, and stories have highly complex effects on the brain—effects that differ from day to day and from person to person. The findings about oxytocin and narrative are validated by Dr. Zak's laboratory work, but much of the rest of it is extrapolation and his educated guesses.

Second, it is not my desire to create a formula that every novel has to follow. My hope is that a basic knowledge of what's going on in the brain will help us be intentional in how we write what we write, with the goal of achieving and maintaining reader engagement.

For example, we've already examined the "rule" to start a novel with action—well, what if there's a brain science reason for why that tends to work? Should we avoid something that works just to avoid the accusation that we're following a formula? Who is going to read a novel that hasn't captured his attention?

So, with all that said, let's begin.

ENGAGE TRANSPORTER

Humans learn through story. Since the beginning of our history, we have sat spellbound as someone like Grandpa Og tells the story of how his own father was eaten by a saber-toothed tiger because he went out alone and unarmed at dusk.

It's a cautionary tale, of course, but the really wonderful thing about it is that the listeners can imagine that they themselves are Og's hapless pa and can apply the lesson to their own lives: "Wow, I guess *I* shouldn't go out alone and unarmed at dusk, or I might be eaten, too. Thanks, Gramps; important safety tip."

That bit of mental gymnastics—"If it happened to him, it could happen to me, so I'd better take note"—is at the core of why our brains crave story. Psychologists call this "theory of mind." We surmise that, while someone else has another mind, we can still understand it. We gain life-enhancing, and even life-saving, wisdom from stories. The more narratives we hear and learn from, the safer and happier we'll be.

However, story works only if we believe it could be us out there being hunted by those sharp-toothed devils. If the person in the story seems very unlike who we think we are—maybe goofy Uncle Rogg, who likes to strap himself with bacon and spend the night on the ground far from everyone else—then we won't take the lesson to heart. We won't even really care about the story. Serves him right for being stupid. But make the hero of the story seem like the person hearing the story, and suddenly we're all ears.

It is the storyteller's task to convince the hearers that this could happen to them, too. If you want the hearers to really listen—whether you're delivering life-saving advice or just a good tale—you need them to be able to put themselves in the shoes of the characters, to feel what they feel. In the words of Dr. Zak, "Your job as a writer is to have the reader become the characters."

One principle of engaging storytelling, then, has to be that we cause our readers to connect to one or more characters in the novel in such a way that they (our readers) care about them deeply, almost as if the characters are a manifestation of the readers.

What we're talking about here is something psychologists call *transportation*. (Psychologists discovered this concept through volunteers' self-reports. What Dr. Zak did in the lab was find the neural correlates, what was happening in the brain during transportation.)

When you see a person in peril in a story and you yourself begin showing signs of stress—adrenaline, sweaty palms, increased heart rate (plus an increased rate of turning those pages!)—then transportation has occurred. The reader feels that he, or at least someone he deeply cares about, is in peril. When what's happening to the character has a physical effect on the reader, transportation has happened.

That's what we mean when we say we've been swept away by a story. It's what we are unconsciously (or consciously) looking for whenever we sit down to read a work of fiction: We want to be whisked away to another world. We've somehow made the mental leap that causes us to feel that we ourselves have, or someone we care a great deal about has, been placed into a situation so real that it causes a reaction in our own bodies and minds. It's the vicarious adventure, the simulated peril, we crave.

Transportation is the secret ingredient—arguably the *only* ingredient—involved in reader engagement. So if the great commandment of fiction is to engage your reader from beginning to end, then we need to pay a lot of attention to how to make it happen.

BORRINGGG

Dr. Zak and his team hooked up volunteers to a functional brain imaging device and showed them short animated movies to track the regions of the brain that were most active while watching.

One video, the control video, was a simple animation of a man and his young son walking at the zoo. As you might expect, the participants' brains didn't get too excited about it, and their minds began to wander. "Nothing happens" in the brain, Dr. Zak says, "and people just blank out."

Does this sound like what you experience when you're reading a novel that hasn't grabbed you? Your mind wanders and you don't feel engaged, and eventually you put the book down. That's because transportation hasn't occurred.

The other video was a more emotionally engaging animation about the same man and young son, except this time we find out that the son is dying of cancer but doesn't know it, and the father is trying to play and rejoice with his son while grappling with the grief about what is soon to occur.

If I were a betting man, I'd wager that just reading that sentence was enough to make you go, "Aw! Poor boy! Poor daddy!" Your heart reached out. You began to care. You could imagine what it might be like if you were going through it.

That's transportation.

As you might guess, the volunteers' brains lit up like the Fourth of July when they watched the second video. The two regions that were most active were those associated with "theory of mind," or understanding what others are doing, *and* those rich in oxytocin receptors—and oxytocin makes us feel empathy.

Something about one video made the viewers engage strongly, where something about the other video did not. The effective one had (1) emotional content (i.e., compelling characters) and (2) a dramatic structure full of struggle (something interesting happened, as opposed to people simply walking along). These two elements caused the viewer to become engaged with the story. These two elements—which could be summarized as character and plot—allowed the viewer to jump into the skin of someone in the story. Transportation.

Dr. Zak's team took blood draws before and after the video and tested for oxytocin levels in the blood. After the video, they also gave participants the opportunity to give money to a charity related to curing children's cancer. As you might guess, both tests suggested the increased presence of oxytocin in the brains of viewers who watched the more emotional video. The blood test revealed it in a concrete, measurable way, and the charity test revealed it by showing that the people who watched the emotional video were statistically much more inclined to give to the charity than those who had watched the control video.

In other words, *a made-up story actually changed the brain chemistry* of these people, causing them to feel more empathetic toward (i.e., engaged with) fictional characters in a fictional world. Transportation occurred, and science verified it.

Now, one way for us to cause this to occur with our readers is to include a vial of synthetic oxytocin with every novel and instruct them to inhale it one hour before reading. (Dr. Zak and his colleagues actually performed this experiment, and they indeed got more engagement with character and more donations to charity. To read the study's findings, go to www.plosone.org and search for "Oxytocin Increases the Influence of Public Service Advertisements.")

Perhaps a more conventional solution would be to use the same techniques the video used: emotional content and dramatic structure. The former encourages the reader to connect with the characters in the book, and the latter holds the reader's attention long enough for that to happen.

ATTENTION AND EMOTIONAL CONNECTION

Humans are busy little bees. The typical reader of fiction has so many things going on in her life that it's a wonder she can concentrate on anything that takes prolonged attention, like a novel. But that's the magnificence of the healthy brain: It can push aside other matters awhile and allow the person to focus on one thing, like a novel.

Even so, gaining the reader's attention in the first place is tricky, and holding it for four hundred pages is trickier still. Knowing a bit about how the brain works can make this much easier to accomplish.

The primary thing the brain looks for is danger. Am I going to die in the next two seconds? Let's say I'm watching television and a fire breaks out next to me. My brain is going to prioritize my safety. It's going to say, "Who cares if you don't see whether they love it or list it? Get out of here now or die!"

So the trick is to convince your readers that reading your novel is going to save their lives.

Okay, just kidding. (But it's kind of a cool idea. Hmm …)

In a future chapter, we're going to look more closely at how to begin your novel in the way that will best engage your readers' attention based on brain chemistry. So for now I'll simply say that you must use to your advantage the brain's alertness toward danger. Related to this is the brain's continual search for things that are new, unexpected, or previously uncategorized. Surprise, in other words. So to engage your reader at the beginning, you must catch his attention, which you do through dramatic danger or surprise.

Once you have your reader's attention, your every effort should be spent in holding his attention and causing him to become transported.

Transportation is the key. The long-term success of your novel, at least in terms of reader engagement, depends on your ability to maintain his attention long enough for him to emotionally identify with your characters (transportation). Once you've achieved transportation, he is putty in your hands.

The more effective video in Dr. Zak's experiment had emotionally compelling content and a dramatic structure (something happened), as opposed to the ineffective video, which was a nonstructured, tension-free status update about two people at the zoo.

A quote from the movie *Three Amigos!* is relevant here (but really, when *isn't* a quote from *Three Amigos!* relevant?):

> All the great Amigo pictures had one thing in common: Three wealthy Spanish landowners who fight for the rights of peasants. Now, that's something everyone likes. It's a people idea. It's a story a nation can sink its teeth into. But then came *Those Darn Amigos*. A box office failure. Nobody went to see it. Because nobody cares about three wealthy Spanish landowners on a weekend in Manhattan. We strayed from the formula, and we paid the price.

Whatever else you gain from *The Irresistible Novel,* I hope you will resolve to use interesting conflict and emotional content to gain your readers' attention and hold it long enough for transportation to occur. Let's look more at how to do that.

Chapter 22

CHARACTER BRAIN—PLOT BRAIN

In the previous chapter, we saw that two components are necessary to create transportation, which is the secret to reader engagement: compelling characters and a plot rich in struggle. Let's look more at what brain science can tell us about achieving each one.

TRANSPORTING THROUGH CHARACTERS

Have you ever met a stranger—say, sitting beside you on an airliner—and been able to engage so well with that person that, by the time you reach your destination, you are friends who are willing to stay in contact? (Interesting side note: Dr. Zak actually met his future wife on an airplane.) Have you ever been in a crisis with a group of strangers—during a forest fire that is causing the evacuation of homes, for example—and been able to form a working bond with them sufficient to enable you to accomplish feats that would've been impossible for you to accomplish on your own?

Even if you haven't encountered such situations yourself, I'm guessing you can imagine yourself doing so … which is exactly what we're talking about here.

Humans have the ability to quickly connect with other humans, even strangers. It's what allows us to engage in large-scale cooperation. When you learn about a stranger's origins, life situation, knowledge base, occupation, and such, you cease to be strangers, and a relationship is born. And when you find things that connect the two of you, like similar interests or mutual experiences, you feel a kinship that goes beyond what you feel for mere passersby.

What are characters in a novel but strangers? You don't know them from Adam and Eve. You feel no connection to them at the outset.

Now, the potential for you to form an exceedingly close connection to one or more of these people is there. It's there in spades. Indeed, when a reader comes to a novel, she's very much hoping to find someone in those pages with whom she can form a firm bond. She's one half of a relationship in utero, waiting to be born. She's reaching out tendrils of love toward the novel. It's the writer's job to throw out tendrils, too, from the characters to the reader. She'll catch them, to be sure.

"We *want* to be taken into these worlds," Dr. Zak says. "All for twenty dollars, with no airplane flight and no risk to our lives or health or happiness, we can travel worlds away in our brains."

Humans have a strong capability to feel empathy toward others. There is an "emotional simulation" we give out that makes us believe that what someone else is going through is something we can feel, too. To build reader connection to your characters, especially your main character, all you have to do is make that reader think, *Oh, I know what that feels like! Poor guy! Come on, buddy, you can do it!*

In my previous books for Writer's Digest, I've spent whole chapters developing methods for creating a bond between your reader and your protagonist. I didn't have the benefit of Dr. Zak's brain science findings at the time, but it's amazing how I was mirroring the material. Now I know why it works.

You don't have to use sympathy as the only means of connecting your reader to your main character. That was just one example. You can also have a hero who arouses our affection through her humor, generosity, kindness, intelligence, or other traits.

The thing to keep in mind is the goal: causing the reader to feel that the character is like him. When he can imagine himself in your hero's shoes, to the point that he's feeling what she's feeling, you've created transportation, and he's yours.

A Chink in the Armor

The secret to this is *vulnerability.* Neuroscience tells us that, when we perceive vulnerability in others, the brain releases oxytocin. When we see someone who needs help, who admits his imperfections, oxytocin gushes out. Oxytocin is the chemical that causes us to feel empathy.

Storytellers have discovered this by trial and error over the centuries. As I say in my other books, it's no accident that many Disney protagonists are lacking one or both parents (Tarzan, Mowgli, Ariel, Cinderella, Aladdin, Belle, etc.). When you see someone who is lacking or needy or vulnerable, you want to reach out to that person. And voilà, transportation.

So if you want to connect your reader to your hero, and I'm pretty sure you do, show her as vulnerable, incomplete, or in need of comfort.

It is possible to go too far in attempting to create sympathy for a character in fiction. If you cross the line from an active hero who faces setbacks to a passive sad sack character—and dear ol' Charlie Brown comes right up to that line—you can turn reader compassion into reader disdain.

That's why heroes also have to be *active* to be compelling. "In our studies, we have created heroes who don't go anywhere [emotionally]," Dr. Zak says, "and the brain loses interest. The hero has to be, well, heroic. And human. The hero robot is a hard sell. After all, some of the best *Star Trek* episodes are the ones featuring the robot-like Mr. Spock or the android Data behaving with the full range of human emotions. Most of the time, though, it is the human who prevails in stories. That's because the hero with faults and shortcomings is more appealing. They are like us."

The brain wants stories that are uniquely human. It wants human themes, emotional themes, like loss, longing, and love. The key here is to recognize that a successful story, from a neurological viewpoint, is deeply emotional. That's why stories about robots or animals have difficulty hooking readers. The few stories like this that we love are ones that personify (humanize) the nonhuman characters by imbuing human emotions on them. Consider *Charlotte's Web, WALL-E,* or *The Lion King.*

TRANSPORTING THROUGH PLOT

There is one story the brain loves, one tale that rises above all others and engages the brain like no other. I'm not referring to Joseph Campbell's hero's journey, though I will discuss that in a future chapter. I'm talking about something much simpler and more general.

The one story the brain loves above all others is the story of *struggle.*

We love a story of human struggle in which a hero overcomes obstacles and foes in an ordeal that is both outward and inward. At the climax, the protagonist looks deep inside himself and is transformed into a hero who uses his newfound wisdom to overcome crisis.

This is why stories in which nothing "big" happens do not typically succeed. (Big can be in the eyes of the character, even if it's not large in any outward sense.) Without conflict, tension, or stakes—all elements of *struggle*—there is nothing for the brain to get excited about. Which makes it bored.

"Fiction is a simulation of human struggle," Dr. Zak says. "Fiction is the lie that reveals truth. A story girds us for our own struggles. Readers get the vicarious benefit of it almost as strongly as if they'd been through it themselves. The evolutionary psychology of stories suggests that there are universal themes of struggle and overcoming obstacles that nearly always resonate with readers."

If you want your reader to connect with your novel, and I'm pretty sure you do, put your hero into a struggle that feels common to people. Readers will see it as something they have gone through—

or might go through—and will put themselves into that story world. Again, voilà, transportation.

Dr. Zak recommends Gustav Freytag's dramatic arc: exposition, rising action, climax, falling action, and denouement. You and I might look to three-act structure or the hero's journey, or some other story shape, but we can agree that the general shape should be struggle leading to resolution, preferably via the hero's transformation.

MALE AND FEMALE READERS

Ever wonder why there seem to be more female readers of fiction than male? According to surveys conducted in the U.S., Canada, and Britain, men account for only twenty percent of the fiction market.[1]

It's largely because of brain chemistry, it turns out.

"Generally, women release more oxytocin than men for the same stimuli," Dr. Zak says. "That's why women are typically more agreeable. They want to be liked, but they also have that maternal instinct. They are therefore more receptive to oxytocin." This means that women may be more eager to find outlets for all that oxytocin, and it may be why more women enjoy novels than men do.

As for men? "Testosterone actually blocks emotional engagement. That's why men like action movies with cardboard characters. However, when men get in committed, long-term romantic relationships, testosterone falls. It makes them more nurturing. The chick flick they wouldn't have watched a year ago is now okay, and in five years, after they have kids, they'll be the biggest criers at movies."

Because of this, we need a variety of stories and storytellers, he says. "That's why we need multiple artists—because people are at different places chemically. And even though there's only one universal story, there are lots of ways to tell it."

---

1. www.npr.org/templates/story/story.php?storyId=14175229, accessed 7/22/14.

SUMMARY

Your reader's brain is hungry for your story. She stands ready to leap into the shoes of your main character (and other characters besides). All you have to do is show her that the character is like her and is vulnerable, and the oxytocin will flow, making her feel connected and empathetic.

Your reader also stands ready to like your story. But it has to look like it's going to go somewhere and do something. If it feels static or lacks tension, her brain will classify it as not worth her attention. Show her it's going to be a story of struggle, and her brain will become engaged.

Chapter 23
A BRAIN CHEMISTRY STORY MAP

In this chapter, I'm going to walk through a novel from beginning to end, suggesting ways to use the principles of brain chemistry to help you at each stage. That does not mean it's a formula. Every story has a beginning, a middle, and an end, but that's not a formula either. Experiment with these ideas, but don't feel bound by them.

Dr. Zak was pretty much horrified when I told him I wanted something like a brain chemistry story map. That's because we can observe and theorize about what's going on in a reader's mind when he is enjoying a story—and we might even be able to (eventually) figure out which neurotransmitters are being released at certain moments during that reading event. But that doesn't mean we'd understand it or be able to do it intentionally.

"I think this is where the art beats the science," Dr. Zak says. "Writers have deep intuitions on how to engage readers and how to do this across genres, but the science of what happens step by step, which would allow one to reverse engineer the process, simply isn't there." Yet.

I give a story outline below, but it's not prescriptive, it's *descriptive* (it's what may be going on inside the reader's brain when reading certain points of the story). It's Dr. Zak's best guess. So we'll view it in that light and see if we can add our own experimentation and do some narrative science of our own.

GLUTA-OXY-GABA-WHAT?

Dr. Zak's neurological interpretation of Gustav Freytag's dramatic arc goes like this: "It starts with something new and surprising, and increases tension with difficulties that the characters must overcome, often because of some failure or crisis in their past. That leads to a climax where the characters must look deep inside themselves to overcome the looming crisis, and once this transformation occurs, the story resolves itself."

It's pretty standard stuff for those of us who have studied fiction. Where it gets interesting is where he begins guessing about what brain chemicals are active when someone is reading a novel she finds engaging. Remember, (1) these are guesses, and (2) they may be active in the reader's mind, but we may or may not be able to cause them to happen in our readers. Still, it's fun to look at.

The phases are the steps in Freytag's dramatic arc:

- **OPENING:** dopamine, adrenaline
- **RISING ACTION:** on and off dopamine and adrenaline, on and off spikes of oxytocin and testosterone
- **CLIMAX:** adrenaline, glutamate, and then GABA (γ-Aminobutyric acid)
- **FALLING ACTION:** GABA, oxytocin
- **DENOUEMENT:** GABA, serotonin

If you're like me, you may need a primer on what those chemicals do and how they make a person feel when they're released in the brain.

- Dopamine makes you feel good; it's associated with attention and pleasure.
- Adrenaline is associated with threat and crisis; it makes you pay attention.
- Oxytocin makes you feel love, empathy, and willingness to help.
- Testosterone provides drive, motivation, and aggression; it makes you willing to take risks.

- Glutamate is a brain chemical active in learning.
- GABA (γ-Aminobutyric acid) makes you feel calm and relieved.
- Serotonin makes you feel happy and whole; it contributes to memory.

So let's look at Dr. Zak's hypothetical map again. A person reading a novel he likes is feeling excited and a little tense at the opening, which is a good feeling. Very soon, he's beginning to see that he's not at all unlike the character in the novel, which causes him to feel connected to him in a way he can't really explain. Now, when the hero gets into danger, our reader gets sweaty palms and feels a kinship stress, and when the hero is feeling good, so is our reader. The hero faces a monumental struggle, to which our reader can relate, but the hero's drive to succeed makes our reader feel strong and determined, too.

The tension keeps rising in our reader as the hero approaches the climax of the story. The sweaty palms are back, and the pages are being turned like crazy. When the hero has his epiphany, our reader enters into that moment as well and feels as if he has learned something, too—and maybe he has. As soon as the tension is resolved, he feels awash in relief, which continues through to the end of the book, as the author ties everything off.

After sharing such a rousing adventure with the hero, and after overcoming all the struggles, our reader feels all warm and fuzzy about the hero, about some of the other characters in the book, and ultimately about his own place in the world.

This seems like a pretty awesome experience. I've not really thought through my mental states as I've been reading a good novel or watching a good movie, but I suspect it's pretty much as Dr. Zak has theorized.

Let's do that to our readers, too.

THE BEGINNING

Many of Dr. Zak's insights about brain chemistry and story have to do with how to engage the reader at the beginning of a story, so we'll spend most of our time talking about the opening.

The chief goal of the novelist is to engage the reader from beginning to end. That is our great and only commandment. Neuroscience tells us that engagement is transportation—causing the reader to so connect with the main character that she feels the story is happening to *her*—and a story of struggle. Transportation and the presentation of struggle are our goals.

At the beginning of our novels, therefore, we need to (1) start connecting the reader with the hero and (2) show that the story is going to involve tension and struggle, obstacles and foes. We want adrenaline and oxytocin flowing, which will result in the release of dopamine.

Yes, we're hacking our readers' brains. But it's what they want. And if they learn something as a result of reading our novels, and tell others to read them, too, then it's a win all around.

Surprise, Surprise

As we've seen, the brain is constantly on the lookout for danger and the new. If something isn't dangerous, new, or noteworthy in some other way, we get bored and move on.

It stands to reason, then, that a novel that doesn't begin with something dangerous, new, or noteworthy is not likely to gain the attention of any reader. His brain will just say, "Boring! Move on."

That's definitely my experience in trying to read certain novels. If I'm not hooked right away, I put the book down, as we saw in chapter eight. Not enough time in my life to read novels that don't engage me.

What I didn't realize was that I wasn't hooked by the book because it was causing no adrenaline, dopamine, or oxytocin to be released in my brain. It seems my brain is looking for these chemical rushes when I pick up a novel, whether I know it or not, and if I don't begin to get high on them right away (if you'll excuse the metaphor), I'm quickly off to find something else that might hook me up.

"We have evidence for the value of a 'hot open,' so that attention is focused on the story from the beginning," says Dr. Zak. "The hot open—something that grabs the reader's attention in the very beginning, a set piece that makes you know you need to pay attention—gets the reader's attention to a level that allows engagement."

If a story feels predictable and safe, he says, the reader's brain loses interest.

How do you gain a reader's attention? Possibly through action, tension, and conflict. "What's good is an opening that grabs you by the metaphorical throat and won't let go until you turn the page and get more," Dr. Zak says. "It is exciting and engaging and makes you want to figure out what is going on." But it doesn't have to be a car chase or explosion or any other sort of traditional action to gain and keep a reader's attention. "Jane Austen did this quite well using emotional danger or risk," Dr. Zak observes.

Remember that while the brain does pay attention to danger—even danger to a fictional person, which may be why the action opening works—it is also attracted to the new or different.

"The brain is a meaning-making organ," Dr. Zak says. "It does this by finding patterns in the world (even a world of words) and deriving causal relationships from these patterns. When the information it gathers does not fit the known pattern, the attentional circuits motivate us to get more information."

In other words, if you surprise or even slightly confuse the reader, you pique his interest. "The brain takes notice when something is uncertain or disconnected or doesn't make sense. The brain's attentional circuits perk up when it encounters a non sequitur, which might be something verbal or unexpected in a scene." The brain wants to be surprised, captivated by something new or unexpected.

"The risk, of course," Dr. Zak says, "is being so odd that the reader feels he cannot map from his memories [make sense of what's going on], because then the reader stops reading. So a novel's opening must be unusual but not unbelievable or incomprehensible." Our goal should be to make the reader curious enough to find out more but not so baffled that she feels incapable of understanding it.

I once read an unpublished novel in which a teacher was presenting a lesson to a class, and then in the next scene this teacher was in Africa witnessing a man's body being catapulted across the highway. It was unexpected, certainly, and there was danger in that second scene. But the collision of elements was so baffling and troubling that I found it hard to continue reading. Surprise pushed too far results in confusion.

One of Dr. Zak's favorite novels is *Tropic of Cancer* by Henry Miller. In the course of our interviews together, Dr. Zak went back and reviewed what made Miller's opening so compelling to him that he remembered it decades after having last read it.

"I reread the opening to *Tropic of Cancer,* and I found that my memory had conflated the first two paragraphs into one. But Miller's real opening is even better than I had remembered: 'I am living at the Villa Borghese. There is not a crumb of dirt anywhere, nor a chair misplaced. We are all alone here and we are dead.' There are so many beautiful dichotomies here: living/dead, alone/together, crumb/wealth, etc. How could I (sort of) remember this paragraph after thirty years? It imprinted on my brain, it was that good. Of course, we're not all Henry Millers (thank God!), but this is something to shoot for."

Hold Until Adhesive Sets

You gain your reader's attention in the way we've just discussed. If you don't signal to the reader's brain that this book is going to be worth her attention, she'll take her attention elsewhere.

However, our end goal here is not attention but transportation. We can't get to transportation if we don't secure the reader's attention, but the latter is a means to achieving the former. Your book has to hold the reader's attention until transportation has occurred.

"From a storytelling perspective," Dr. Zak says, "the way to keep a reader's attention is to continually increase the tension in the story."

Meanwhile, you're also showing all the many ways that the character (or characters) in your story is like the reader and is vulnerable. You're doing two things at once: holding the reader's attention, through tension, and building transportation so the reader will jump into the hero's shoes.

"Once a story has sustained our attention long enough," Dr. Zak says, "we may begin to emotionally resonate with the story's characters. Narratologists call this *transportation*, and you experience it when your palms sweat as James Bond trades blows with a villain on top of a speeding train."

(By the way, I don't know what a narratologist is, but I think I want to be one.)

Our goal is reader engagement. The key to reader engagement is transportation, with a side order of struggle. Through the surprising and perhaps dangerous situations we're using to gain and keep the reader's attention, we're showing that it will be a story of struggle, full of obstacles, tension, and enemies. But it's all in service to the real goal, which is to cause your reader to cease being a reader at all and to start being the hero in your novel.

How long do you have to sustain the reader's attention before he has been transported into the skin of your hero? I have no idea. Neither does Dr. Zak. It can happen very quickly, as when you may have felt your emotions stirring when I simply told you about a man trying to play with his son despite knowing his son was about to die of cancer. That was just one sentence, and you were already beginning to experience transportation!

If you create an opening scene of eight to fifteen pages, showing what's human and likeable and compelling about your main character and pitting her against a variety of obstacles, I'd be willing to bet that your reader will be well on his way to making the leap. Especially if you're being intentional about it.

PERSPECTIVE

Let's take a minute to step back and look at what we're talking about. There's really nothing new or surprising in what we're learning. Start with something interesting, connect your reader to your protagonist, etc. It's more like finding out that there's scientific support for something we're already doing.

When I began this brain chemistry research, I half expected to find something bizarre, like the secret to engaging the reader was to include a purple zebra in every novel. It's comforting to know that the things I've been teaching writers and doing in my own fiction for years are actually borne out by the science.

It's also yet another tool that helps us evaluate the various "rules" of fiction. If someone tells me I'm not supposed to use certain words in my fiction, I can stand that up next to our great commandment (engaging the reader from beginning to end) and the neurological goal of transportation and go, "Yeah, that really has no bearing, so I'm going to forget I heard it."

THE MIDDLE

A good story, as we've seen, starts with something arresting, then increases tension. But you can't keep the pedal to the metal all the time. The brain can't stay in fight-or-flight mode endlessly, or it will begin having other, undesirable, side effects. Turns out that the line of your story shouldn't be so much a diagonal leading straight up to the climax but rather a wiggly, hilly line with lots of ups and downs.

Our task is to balance tension (needed in order to retain the reader's attention) with rests and waypoints (needed to allow the tension to become effective again), during a novel's dreaded sagging middle.

"Boredom creeps in easily," Dr. Zak notes. "Being able to get someone to continue to turn pages is nearly miraculous. The brain wants the 'new, new thing,' and writers have to convince readers that that new, new thing is to be found on the next page, the next chapter. If a story seems predictable and safe, we lose interest."

But what about transportation? If we've done our job right at the beginning, then we've engaged our reader. He's put himself into the shoes and life of the hero. Putty in our hands, right? Um, not necessarily.

"Yes," Dr. Zak says, "when transportation occurs, the reader has been captured by the writer. But the narrative can devolve so that transportation is lost."

In other words, it's possible to get your reader on the hook but not be able to reel him in. Where that usually happens is in the middle. From a brain science perspective, your two best tools for keeping your reader engaged in the middle of your novel are anticipation and the sine wave.

Anticipation

We love to have our curiosity aroused. When we're intrigued about something, our brains gush out dopamine, making us feel like we've won the lottery. Or, rather, that we might be *about* to win the lottery.

Novelists can put this aspect of brain science to use in their books. "What makes a story work is that inescapable need for the brain to know what is going to happen next," Dr. Zak says. "That's what keeps us awake at night reading. Curiosity is aroused. Your survival instincts kick in. It's a drug—literally. A dopamine rush."

How do you keep your reader hooked on the dopamine you're dealing? By use of anticipation. "The brain loves anticipation and discovery and finding clues," Dr. Zak says, citing as examples *The Da Vinci Code* and every Robert Ludlum book ever written.

The brain's motivation system *loves* anticipation. It loves it even more than the arrival of what is anticipated. "This is why compulsive gamblers love to hit the tables. They're hoping that this time, just this time, they will win. Then if they ever do win, they are perplexed." It wasn't the winning they were hoping for, truly. The chase, the hunt, the challenge—the anticipation—was what they were really after.

A great way to keep the middle of your book from sagging, from causing the reader's brain to lose interest, is to keep doling out the clues and the hints. Give the reader a crumb. Disclose a little more about the mystery. Move the hero a bit closer to figuring out what's going on.

You can also use anticipation on a broader scale with the ticking time bomb literary device. This is the immovable deadline affecting the hero's activities, after which the opportunity to act will be over. It's the asteroid hurtling toward Earth or the volcano about to erupt or the dam about to burst or the ship about to hit the iceberg. (Or just the end of the song, after which the girl won't be willing to reconcile with the boy, so he'd better hurry up.)

The reader knows it's coming and that it can't be avoided. It's not even really important that the characters in the book know it's coming. What you want to do is the equivalent of having the horror moviegoer yell at the screen, "Don't go in there!"

Planting a ticking time bomb at the base of your story, figuratively speaking, is a terrific way to amp up the anticipation, especially in the middle stretches of your novel.

Consider the movie *Dante's Peak*. Though the volcano didn't erupt until deeper in the movie, the first half of the film gave sign after sign that the eruption was rapidly drawing nearer. With each of those reminders—especially the ones that happened in the middle of the story—the viewer's anticipation went up and up and up. It would be difficult to get bored in a movie when you realize that a volcano could go off, killing characters you've come to care about, at any moment.

Consciously use anticipation and curiosity and tension throughout your book, not just in the middle but especially there, to keep your reader on the hook.

The Sine Wave

The brain needs rest stops. Breaks. You can't keep ramping up and ramping up, or it eventually becomes too exhausting to maintain, and the reader is forced to stop. In general, we don't want to force our readers to stop reading.

"The brain can't sustain high tension forever," Dr. Zak says. Pretty soon, "it needs a tension relief. Cutting away to another storyline will help here, as will humor. The brain needs to take a breather. It's a sine wave with peaks and valleys. As the writer, you're balancing tension with emotional resonance. The break, feeling a bit of relief and joy, lets the reader build back up our attentional resources to give you again."

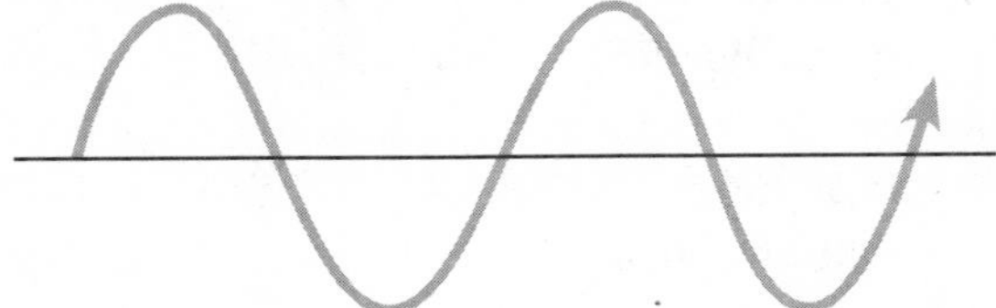

"Even suspense novels need neural rest points," Dr. Zak says. "These could be comic relief, or the resolution of a shorter storyline, or the protagonist's survival from an evil plot. Rests and beats are important."

It's no accident that Shakespeare's tragedies have some brilliant comic characters. Juliet's nurse is a prime example. We laugh at her malapropisms and overall manner, and boy, do we need those respites from the unrelenting tragedy mounting up around us.

In a way, Shakespeare was actually crueler to us by including little laugh breaks. Because they allow our brains to rest a bit, that allows us to receive more sorrow. Had we not had the little chuckle, and the resulting neurotransmitter release, we might've said, "Enough!" and walked out to gain back some balance in our brains. But Shakespeare did give us a laugh now and then, curse him, and so we stay to receive helping after helping of sadness.

Let's target a sine wave structure for the middle section of our novel. It's a slanted sine wave, you recall: heading generally up toward the climax. Just not in a straight line. More like this:

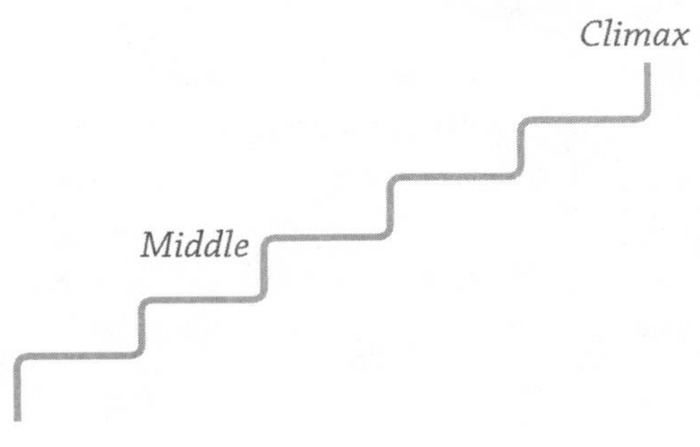

Most novelists include this sort of thing by instinct—even as writers we can't maintain the intensity for a whole book. It just feels wrong somehow. Now we know why.

If your novel can have more than one storyline going, that can be your primary way of managing this rhythm. Take one storyline to a cliffhanger, and then cut away to another storyline that is in a calmer state. Not only will you give the reader's brain a needed break, you'll also be increasing anticipation ("Please get back to that other storyline!"), thus keeping your reader on the hook in two ways.

We've already mentioned comic relief. Maybe you feel good about including humor in your fiction, and maybe you don't. If it makes you nervous, you don't have to use it. But you might give it a try. There are dozens of forms of humor that can be done in fiction, and I'll bet one or more of them would be doable for you. Your reader needs some levity alongside the heaviness.

The opposite is true as well. If your novel is primarily light and funny, sprinkling in some legitimately serious bits will help your reader go back to laughing it up.

The middle of your novel needs to be generally trending toward your final confrontation, but it's hard to keep the reader's brain engaged the whole time. Use the power of anticipation, curiosity, and the almighty sine wave to keep him running with you to the big finish.

CLIMAX AND DENOUEMENT

You've grabbed your reader's attention, you've shown her a story of human struggle, you've caused her to be transported into the body of your hero, you've kept her on the hook through anticipation and breaks and respites, you've ramped the tension up and up, and now you're ready to tackle the climax of the book.

There are three things the brain is looking for in the climax and resolution of a story: transformation, resolution of the problem, and a good outcome for the hero.

First, the reader needs the hero to be transformed. She must look deep inside herself, realize how she must change to become who she needs to be, and embrace the change. In my teaching, I call this the moment of truth in the protagonist's inner journey. Everything in the story has been in service to this decision.

Now, you can have the protagonist choose the "wrong" way, the way that leads to destruction, but the reader's brain won't be happy with you. The reader's brain wants the main character—who is, you'll recall, the reader's own surrogate now—to make the right choice, to learn her lesson and step onto the path of life. If she does, the reader himself will feel that he has learned as well (remember GABA?).

For the sake of your reader's brain, I encourage you to put your hero on an inner journey of transformation that leads her to a moment of truth in which she decides to choose the "right" way. (I cover the inner journey at length in *Plot Versus Character* and my other Writer's Digest books.)

Second, the climax must resolve the main problem plaguing the characters of the book. If your novel is about escaping a bus that will blow up if it ever drops below forty miles per hour, and you end by having the hero decide he really is going to go back and finish college after all, your reader's brain will not like you. You've got to get him off the bus first. Then you can think about college.

"We have tested narratives in which the climax does not resolve the dilemma," Dr. Zak says, "and there is a sort of brain confusion, because the pattern is broken. This results in reader disengagement. The climax is the tension reliever. It should feel satisfying."

Your climactic moment will feel satisfying to the reader if you're sure to resolve the main problem presented in the story.

Third, your reader's brain really does want a happy ending for the hero. This is probably true for two reasons. For one thing, if you've done your job well (and your reader wouldn't have reached the end of the novel if you haven't), the reader has *become* the hero in your book. Most people desire a positive future for themselves. This reader feels that she's just been through the wringer with your hero, so of course she wants it to work out well, exactly as she wants things to work out well for herself.

For another thing, even if the reader doesn't feel she *is* the hero, she at least *likes* the hero, and we always want good things to come to people we care about. Your story has caused her brain to release oxytocin, which has made her connect emotionally with your hero. She's become so invested in this fictional person that she'd be willing to take "costly action" for her, as Dr. Zak discovered with the experiment about giving to a children's cancer charity. When you invest yourself in helping someone succeed, you quite naturally want to see that person succeed.

When a novel causes us to connect that deeply to a character and then some great misfortune befalls that character, we're going to be mad at the author. Our brains hurt. We worked hard, or so we feel, to bring about this person's success, and the author didn't let that happen. Bad idea, in my opinion.

That doesn't mean your war novel has to end with the hero dancing in the streets of Paris. A main character can suffer harm or even die and it will still feel like a happy ending to the reader if that's the "right" and satisfying resolution for that character. Consider Théoden's demise in *The Return of the King*. He dies, by gum, but the reader feels satisfied—happy, even—because of how pleased Théoden is with how he's comported himself. He dies with honor, and we're glad to see him go as he wished to go.

SUMMARY

Neurology has given us enough of a peek into how the ol' noodle works to begin to help the novelist accomplish the only essential task of any novel, which is to keep the reader engaged from beginning to end.

Attract the reader's attention through the dangerous and the new. Show a hero in a struggle everyone can relate to. Give the reader chances to do what she wants to do already—form a tight, skin-to-skin bond with your hero. Ratchet up the tension on the way to your story's climax, using anticipation, curiosity, and little breaks and rests. Send your hero on a journey of discovery and transformation, and at the apex of the story, have him reach deep and embrace his change. In a whirlwind of tension and action, let the hero confront and overcome the final foe or obstacle, resulting in an ending that rewards the reader's efforts to help this hapless one you've put through so much drama.

Your reader's brain is flowing with neurochemicals as she reads your novel. By how you organize your story, those chemicals will either draw your reader closer to your book or push her away. Not concentrating on them won't make them any less potent, any less forceful in determining your reader's opinion of the book. So if these chemicals are behind whether your reader loves your novel, I'd say you ought to consider using them to your advantage. I know I'm going to.

Chapter 24

WHAT'S IT ALL ABOUT, ALFIE?

For years, I've trained novelists how to write better fiction. My set of teachings came from observations of what seemed to work for me—in my own fiction—and *on* me as a reader of fiction and a viewer of film and TV narratives.

Over the years my opinions and stances on various aspects of fiction craftsmanship have changed a bit here or there. Mostly I've become more mellow about the "rules" of fiction (as Part One of this book shows pretty well!), going from being adamant about some of them to stepping back to a position of "This is what I find effective for me, but if you want to do it another way, that's fine."

It's been a matter of changing my focus from the trees to the forest. There are dozens of techniques I find vital for my own writing. I feel they are the most effective ways of accomplishing my goals in fiction. But I've come to see them as trees, as nonessentials, as tools only, and not *the ultimate secret.* They're still great and I still use them, but if somebody wants to not use them, that fiction can be successful as well.

The thing that rocked my convictions about fiction was the repeated evidence that best-selling novels could break every rule I found essential and violate every technique I found pivotal. And then be made into movies. Apparently, what I considered great fiction craftsmanship didn't amount to a hill of beans in this crazy world.

Novels I saw with astounding craftsmanship would sometimes sell well, but most times they did not. Novels I saw with horrific craftsmanship would often fail miserably, but some of them shot the moon. Some of both kinds did well, actually, and some of both kinds did poorly. In other words, high or low fiction craftsmanship didn't seem to make the slightest difference in how well a novel sold.

That's a lot to drop on the head of a guy who has spent his career teaching fiction craftsmanship.

I feel like the medieval physician who finally figures out that bleeding a patient with leeches is just as likely to kill him as cure him, and that bleeding a patient plays no part at all in health. The whole system is built upon a faulty foundation. So what are he and his fellow physicians *doing?*

If high fiction craftsmanship isn't the secret to making a novel wildly popular, what is?

I concluded that it has everything to do with whether the novel engages the reader. If a novel captivates the reader and keeps him enthralled until the final page, that is a novel with a chance for commercial success.

When I made that realization, my whole attitude toward teaching fiction changed. I saw that there was no need to be adamant about this technique or that rule. Indeed, I suddenly understood that the emphasis on technique was misplaced.

That's not to say that good fiction craftsmanship doesn't contribute to reader engagement, because I wholeheartedly believe it does. I have a whole raft of techniques I cling to because I believe they are highly effective at keeping the reader gripped. A novelist still has tools in her kit, after all, even if the focus has shifted from the tools themselves to the overall effectiveness of the thing being built.

Nor is it to say that rules have no place in fiction. The beginning writer, especially, craves rules, as we have seen. So I see my previous teaching on fiction craft as useful as a means to start writers out well. But now I quickly shift the focus to reader engagement.

So when I discovered Dr. Paul J. Zak and his studies on brain chemistry and engagement with story, I knew I had to investigate. If reader engagement is the only essential for successful fiction, and if there might be a scientific means of achieving reader engagement,

I wanted to be all over it. And if it meant trading some of my trial and error for targeted strategies, I would count myself fortunate.

I have found Dr. Zak's findings and theories to be extremely helpful. They have been and will continue to be effective in my own fiction, and I know I'll get better at implementing them as I continue to use them. It's amazing having this information as a guide and a plan.

But as with anyone who has just embraced a new philosophy, it takes awhile for it to become integrated into all corners of our minds. I've had to step back to see how Dr. Zak's neurological insights about engagement with story mesh with everything else I've been teaching novelists.

So I did a survey of my previous Writer's Digest books. I didn't find anything I needed to change—except perhaps wanting to shift more toward the forest and less toward the trees.

For instance, you still want to begin with something engaging happening, as I've always taught, and now we know why. You still want to be intentional about how you bring your protagonist onstage for the first time, and now we know exactly which things we want to emphasize as we do so (things that will lead to reader transportation). You still want to send your hero on an inner journey that will culminate in her being transformed, and now we know the reader's brain craves this.

It's less about *-ly* adverbs and more about getting the reader to identify with the main character. I stand by the craftsmanship I have taught, but if I had to choose between a consistent POV and something that would cause instant reader transportation, I'm going to go with the brain chemistry over the good use of craft.

Of course, we don't *have* to choose between these two. They're not mutually exclusive. We can employ craftsmanship we can be proud of, craftsmanship we believe will enhance reader engagement, right alongside a masterful use of brain chemistry.

Whatever tools or philosophies we decide to use, if our efforts combine to keep the reader engaged from beginning to end, we have won.

Part Three
THE BRAIN'S GREATEST HITS

"The time for the passing of a threshold is at hand."

—Joseph Campbell, *The Hero with a Thousand Faces*

Once you were freed from the fiction writing rules described in Part One, in Part Two I encouraged you to concentrate on only one goal: keeping your reader engaged from beginning to end. We explored the power of brain chemistry and learned how to intentionally grab the reader's attention.

Now that you're convinced (I hope) that you want to harness the energy of neuroscience for your fiction, in Part Three we'll look at storytelling tools that have withstood the test of centuries. These three systems—Joseph Campbell's monomyth (the hero's journey), Carl Jung's archetypes, and Aristotle's *Rhetoric*—feature narrative elements that have proved effective again and again throughout history. Even though we don't yet have specific brain science explaining why they endure, we know *that* they endure, which means they are doing something vigorous in the ol' noodle. And that's the sort of thing we want to harness for our own novels.

But, you might ask, aren't these elements clichés or formulas, and don't we want to be fresh and original?

If you have a young person going on a journey of self-discovery, then yes, such stories have been told before. Probably this story will have roughly the same stages as other coming-of-age stories.

But there's a difference between being formulaic (as in, uninspired or purposefully derivative) and tapping into metaphors that populate our collective unconscious. These archetypal elements—the mentor, the friend, the mother, the trek, the call to adventure—are archetypes because they resonate with pretty much every human. I don't know if it's even possible to write a story that does *not* tap into some archetypal theme, character, or sequence.

As always, use what parts of this section seem helpful to you and ditch the rest. If you start feeling constrained and paralyzed by these systems, you have my permission to reject them. I want you to feel equipped and energized as you sit down to write the story of your heart.

Chapter 25
THE MONOMYTH

In 1949, mythologist Joseph Campbell published *The Hero with a Thousand Faces,* a seminal book revealing the synthesis of his studies of comparative mythology from human civilizations all over the world and across time. The central thesis of the book is that there is one story, one megamyth, that occurs in a thousand forms but according to a set pattern in the lore of every human culture.

He called it the monomyth. We know it as the hero's journey.

While the neuroscience may not yet be there to prove why the monomyth resonates within the brain of nearly every person who has ever lived on our planet, I'm willing to go out on a limb and say there's something happening here. If it's that deeply stirring to most everyone in the species, there's a good chance there's a neurological reason for it.

The hero's journey is the classic coming-of-age story, which (most of us would attest) is the ultimate tale of struggle. Stories of struggle are what the brain craves, you'll recall. And if the eponymous hero on the journey is going through the phases of adolescence we all endured, then by definition, he is someone with whom everyone can identify. In that sense, then, the monomyth is the first and most perfect story for giving the brain what it wants in a narrative.

I would be interested in finding out what percentage of Hollywood movies in recent years have been hero's journey stories. I suspect the percentage is high, maybe up to 50 percent. Not every hero's journey story seems to be a coming-of-age tale about adolescence, but every hero's journey story is *essentially* a coming-of-age tale in that the same steps of struggle and mastery are present. And when you add stories that include major elements of the hero's journey arc, I'd guess the percentage would go up from there.

But even so, it's probably not 99 percent, which means there's room for you to tell your non-hero's journey stories as freely as you want. (Folks who don't resonate as well with the hero's journey tale might enjoy Robin Childs's description of "the antagonist's tale" or the villain's story.)

In this chapter, I give a brief overview of the monomyth. As you read, keep in mind everything you learned in Part Two about what the reader's brain is wanting. Whether you follow Campbell's sequence precisely or use just a few elements of it, you can rest assured that you're on solid ground and that your reader's brain will thank you.

As we progress through the hero's journey, you'll see some "stock" characters: the mentor, the shadow, the lover, etc. These are archetypes, which we'll talk more about in the next chapter. In a real sense, the whole monomyth is one giant archetype, which may be further evidence that this story is etched into every reader's brain.

THE SHAPE OF THE JOURNEY

The hero's journey is often graphically depicted as a circle. This there-and-back-again structure is important, because it's essentially the story of our hero's rite of passage. He has one status within the tribe as the story begins: a child (literally or figuratively). He's protected and exempted from the duties of adults, but he also doesn't get the freedoms the adults enjoy. At the end of his journey, if things go as everyone hopes, he will *reintegrate* into the tribe, but with a new status: that of an adult who can begin contributing to the welfare of the tribe.

Lying between "child" and "adult" is the rite of passage. It is the expulsion from safety into a world of supernatural mystery, where the youth must learn how to fend for himself and become a man. This is the initiation phase, and it's where most of the awesomeness happens. It corresponds, as you may have already noticed, to act two in a three-act structure. I'm a big fan of act twos.

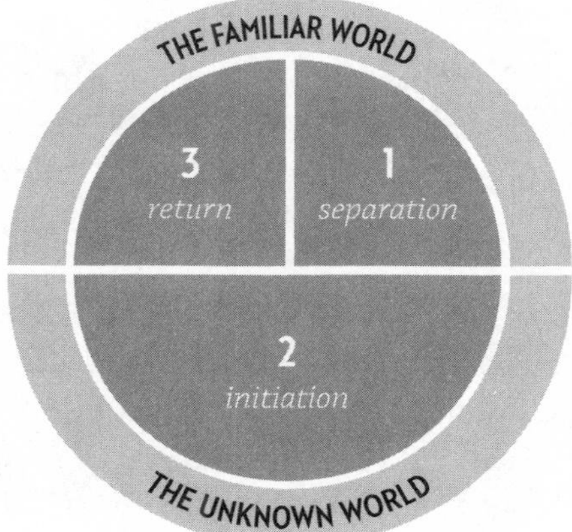

After the child has learned a thing or two, experienced pain, found new foes and friends, and gone through the other steps of initiation, he is ready to return to the village to begin giving to his tribe out of the wealth of his new knowledge, strength, and confidence.

Don't be too literalistic about the percentages represented here. Shift things around to suit your taste. Many hero's journey movies and novels look more like this:

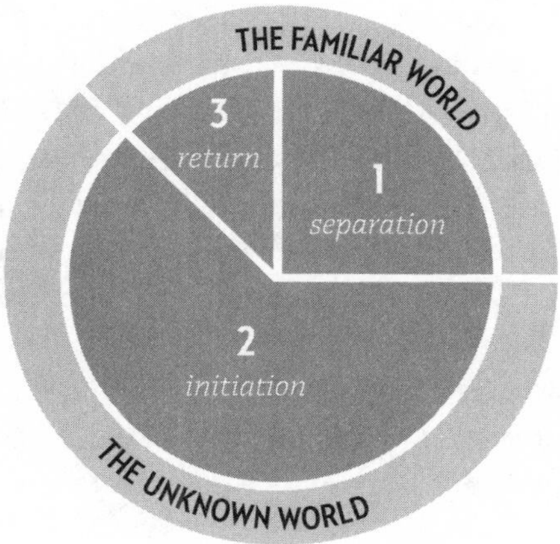

Which, not coincidentally, coincides pretty well with the underlying three-act structure. But you can cut your own pie slices as big or as small as you like to serve your story.

THE ELEMENTS OF THE HERO'S JOURNEY

I don't know of a single movie or novel that uses every one of the hero's journey elements, so don't stress if you'd rather not use all of them. And if you'd like to shuffle them around or change who does what, feel free. The myth stories Campbell drew these elements from were likewise flexible (imbued with glorious fluidity, actually), so you can use them flexibly, too.

With each of the seventeen steps or stages on the journey, I'll give a brief explanation of what it entails and then an example or two from movies or fiction.

By the way, Christopher Vogler has written a book called *The Writer's Journey* that gives one author's interpretation of how to use the monomyth in fiction. You may find it useful as well. (Your best option will be to go to *The Hero with a Thousand Faces,* but it's not exactly a light read.)

The Call to Adventure

The hero (and, by the way, this works for *heroines,* too, so please hear my use of *hero* as gender neutral, even if I go with male pronouns) is living in a protected but boring, mundane, and often bucolic world. The world of childhood, at least metaphorically speaking. It's safe, and the hero may or may not be longing for adventure.

This is Luke Skywalker on the moisture farm or Frodo Baggins in the Shire or Belle (from *Beauty and the Beast*) in her quaint village. Luke wants to go to the Academy and join the rebellion against the Empire. Frodo is quite happy staying where he is, though he does love hearing tales of elves and his Uncle Bilbo's adventures. Belle wants much more than her provincial life.

Into this placid life comes an intrusion from the outside world. It often comes in the form of a herald (Campbell's term for the person who introduces to the hero the idea of going on the journey; in *Mulan,* it's a literal herald calling people to join the Emperor's army), but the harbinger can also be an event. Whatever it is, it suggests to the hero that there is a larger world out there, the unknown, and there may be reason for him to leave his home and go to places off the map.

For Luke, the call to adventure came in the form of two droids who rolled into his family farm and were being pursued by the evil Galactic Empire. For Frodo, it was the passing to him of the Ring of Power. For Ariel (in *The Little Mermaid*), it was her encounter with a sailing ship and a handsome prince that started her thinking about leaving home.

The Refusal of the Call

Some heroes jump right up, link arms with the herald, and sprint toward the unknown world. But many heroes don't. In fact, no matter how bored they've been or how much they've pined that they want *more,* when someone calls their bluff, they may be inclined to decline the opportunity.

Since Frodo never wanted to leave the Shire at all, we can understand why he would want to give this duty to someone else. But Luke ought to be ashamed that when his chance to fight the Empire finally comes, he drags his heels, says, "It's all such a long way from here," and claims that his obligations won't let him go.

Whether it's from a sense of responsibility—"If I leave, who will take care of Grandma?"—or a feeling of inadequacy or whatever else, the child (or initiate) hero may be reluctant to go when the call finally comes.

That doesn't mean the hero gets out of the adventure. It just means he'll either need to be convinced to go or he'll need to be dragged off, kicking and screaming. Either way is fine, because he's going to go. Or else we have no story.

Supernatural Aid

It is said that when the pupil is ready, the master appears. That may be a cliché for us today, but it's true in the monomyth. The hero needs to be assured that destiny has called him onto this journey, and that therefore he will have the strength he needs.

Supernatural aid often comes in the form of the mentor, usually a male teacher figure or guide (at least for male initiates; maybe female heroes need female mentors), who speaks words of affirmation to the hero and may even give him some powerful talisman (light saber, anyone?) to give the hero faith that he might be able to survive the wilds after all.

Campbell says that there is a sense in which the call to adventure was actually the first announcement of the approach of this "initiatory priest," who will guide the hero through the process of becoming a man.

So we have Merlin for Arthur, Gandalf for Frodo, Obi-Wan Kenobi for Luke, Haymitch for Katniss (in *The Hunger Games*), Dumbledore for Harry Potter, the Oracle for Neo (in *The Matrix*), Rufus for Bill and Ted (in *Bill & Ted's Excellent Adventure*), and Mary Poppins.

Encouraged by this new help and armed with his magical sword or wand or amulet, our hero determines to head out into the unknown.

Crossing the First Threshold

At the boundary between the familiar world and the strange lands beyond stands a threshold. Perhaps it's a river that must be crossed or a portal that must be stepped through.

For Frodo, it was the limits of the Shire. For Luke, it was the farm he'd grown up on. For Ariel, it was the edge of the ocean. Whatever the character's mundane life had been, it has extreme outskirts, and that's the threshold he must cross to begin his adventure.

There is almost always a price to be paid for crossing this boundary, and the passage is often blocked by the threshold guardian. In the Bible, when God cast Adam and Eve from the Garden of Eden, he set as guard of the threshold a mighty angel with a flaming sword. Frodo's Shire was surrounded on one side by an ancient and evil forest, which didn't take kindly to anyone passing through it. In order to become human, Ariel faced a species barrier. She needed to become human so she could go to dry land to try to get the prince to fall in love with her. But the only person who could do that was the sea witch, not someone to be bargained with lightly.

The hero may be barred from crossing into the field of adventure, and getting past this guardian is his first test of initiation. Often, though, the threshold guardian possesses wisdom that would aid the hero as he enters into the dangerous world beyond. If the hero has to fight this guardian and prevails, he will inherit some of the guardian's magical ability. Whether he's trying to keep the hero safe (but uninitiated) or to strengthen him for the journey, the guardian seems like a hindrance but is often actually a strong ally.

Crossing the first threshold requires the hero to leave something behind. That may be something tangible like family, a pet, or a village, or it may be intangible like his pride or his childhood or his safety. But something of the old and immature way is sacrificed in the effort to become something larger.

Belly of the Whale

Eight of Campbell's seventeen stages occur in the supernatural realm beyond the familiar world. The preceding four happen in that mundane world, as do the final five, but you can see that the heart of the action happens where the hero is not in Kansas anymore.

Shortly after crossing out of the familiar world, the world of the unknown swallows our hero up. Luke is pulled into the tractor beam of the Death Star. Belle is made a prisoner in the cursed castle of the Beast. Maximus (from *Gladiator*) is made a slave who must fight in the arena again and again to survive long enough to exact his revenge.

Often, the hero enters the belly of the whale (referring to the biblical Jonah story) a victim—possibly a captive or draftee. But what the hero perceives as an unwelcome turn of events is actually the very training he will need to be able to face the ordeals in his future. If he can learn his lessons and discover his strength, he will emerge from the whale no longer victim but victor.

Luke came into manhood inside that ol' metal Death Star. Frodo's experiences in Middle-earth steeled him (and his loyal companion, Sam) for the ultimate test to come. Sherlock Holmes enters the criminal's domain, sometimes in disguise, so that he can solve the crime. Neo leaves the Matrix and enters the real world in order to learn what he has to do to overcome his enemies back in the Matrix.

The hero stepping into the world of the unknown is like a worshipper entering a temple. He sheds who he was, is stripped of his identity, is given new clothes and rites, and becomes something else entirely. The belly of the whale metaphor represents the entire time he's in the outside world, even if he leaves the "whale" shortly after entering. He is consumed and overpowered—sometimes even suffering the loss of a limb or an eye, etc.—but this is in reality the exact path he must take if he is to survive the initiation and become an adult.

Road of Trials

Ah, the quest. The hero must cross the realm or the galaxy or the desert or the ocean or the forest—or the world of high fashion—to get to his goal. The road of trials phase brings the hero a succession of challenges and ordeals, one or more of which he will inevitably fail, that begin to strengthen his transformation.

In a sense, this is the beginning of the initiation proper.

As he's facing these trials (like learning combat, being hurt by new foes, or trying to leap over unimaginable distances), he is aided by his mentor, his new allies, his talisman of power, and/or superhuman support.

As the hobbit Bilbo was fond of saying, "It's a dangerous business, Frodo, going out your door. You step onto the road, and if you don't keep your feet, there's no knowing where you might be swept off to."

Out here are impossible tasks and unexpected allies. Tricksters and friends. Loyalty and betrayal. New rules and new wonders. Each of them will show, harden, or break the hero's determination to continue down this road of trials.

He is being purified and humbled, broken down so that he might be rebuilt as a man. These trials are perfectly suited to equip this hero with the abilities he needs if he is to succeed in the final ordeal to come. The ritual of initiation is carefully crafted with this hero in mind.

Luke wanted to cross the galaxy to rescue a princess, but he really had no idea what that would entail. Frodo was willing to take the Ring to its destruction, but it sounded much more possible when surrounded by allies and the walls of a friendly fortress. Ariel was really a selfish and headstrong girl when she defied her father and set off to win her prince.

In all cases, the task becomes much more difficult, much more serious, than the hero originally thought. So it is in life. There are setbacks and people in line ahead of you and prejudices holding you down. An entire system operating without you and without *need* of you, or so it seems. How can you ever reach your goal?

But along this road of trials there are also new best friends to be made, new caverns of wonder to be discovered, new leaders to support, and best of all, new abilities to be awakened inside the hero.

Meeting with the Goddess

One thing a child (or any uninitiated person) back in the village can't do is marry a beautiful woman. Only adult men who are full members of the tribe can take a wife. Anyway, he knows all the girls his own age from back home, and none of them really thrill him. But out here in the unknown is where his true love lives. Had he stayed home, he never would've even known about her, much less won her heart.

In the unknown realm beyond the borders of his home is where he finds a woman who is his completion, the powerful match for his maturing new self. She is strong and brave and competent. She is a prize to be won by overcoming her many other suitors. She is unattainable and frightening, both mother and destroyer, both womb and tomb. She is all that can be known, but it will take a master to know her, to comprehend her secrets. She is no wilting wallflower, and only a true man can hope to make her his own.

Princess Leia is way out of Luke's league (and he finds out later she is actually his twin sister), but that doesn't stop him from trying. She inspires him to be more than he thought he could be. Ariel can't even speak to Prince Eric (because of a magic spell that took her voice), but she knows in her heart he is the one who will complete her. Trinity was a legendary butt-kicker years before Neo even awoke from the Matrix, but she believes that she is destined to fall in love with "the one," so he'd better live up to that and fulfill his destiny.

A key part of the hero becoming an adult is an awakening of his desire for romantic intimacy. But this is also one of his primary tests of manhood. He must *win* this ultimate, perfect bride. He must prove himself worthy. And that is not done by taking the easy road or by shying away from danger. The meeting with the goddess is both his inspiration to try harder and his reward for doing so. If he can become the ultimate man he can be, then she will gladly be his.

It's one more seemingly impossible challenge, to be worthy of such a woman. Becoming deserving of this "mystical marriage" is "the final test of the talent of the hero to win the boon of love," says Campbell.

Interestingly, the character trait most often associated with the hero's success at being worthy of the goddess is not courage or loyalty or perseverance, but kindness. The gentle heart will win the love of the mighty warrior-goddess.

Woman as the Temptress

His goddess bride may be the whole cosmos to him, but she can also become a temptation. He didn't come out here to enjoy endless intimacy, not even with the perfect woman, but to pass a rite of initiation and return to the village to help the tribe. At some point, according to Campbell, "the world, the body, and woman above all, become the symbols no longer of victory but of defeat."

The hero must become like Galahad, the purest of King Arthur's knights and thus the only one to actually obtain the prize: the Grail. Nothing, no matter how incredible, must be allowed to divert the hero from his true goal.

Sirens sit on rocks in the sea and call sailors to their ruin. In *Monty Python and the Holy Grail* (to go back to Arthur), a castle of sex-starved, beautiful women nearly causes Galahad to abandon his purity and thus forsake the Grail. A life of financial success can cause the hero to forget why he got into this business in the first place. Maverick (in *Top Gun*) falls in love with Charlie (a woman), and it threatens to deprive him of his life's ambition. In *The Empire Strikes Back*, Luke gives in to the temptation to leave his Jedi training to try to save his friends, and it results in disaster.

All of us face temptations. And on the road of trials, when the hero is getting the hang of things in the belly of the whale, he can begin experiencing a level of success with important but secondary matters (and can overcome discouragement) that may almost be enough to lure him away from what should be his focus.

In the end, even a goddess is not enough of a goal in and of itself to sway the hero from his task. He has a calling, a destiny, and while the woman may become his strongest ally in the quest, he must not allow her (or anything else) to become its *object*.

Atonement with the Father

At the center point of the initiation, the hero comes face to face with the most powerful force in his own life, a force that has the ability to give him life or death. Upon this encounter hinges the hero's entire journey.

Often, this force is represented by the hero's father or a father figure. But this is the father in his ogre form: judge and executioner, creator and destroyer.

The test here, curiously, is for the hero to believe that the terrifying face of the father-god is actually a face that can be trusted. It is manhood in all its fury, but manhood whose fury is, despite evidence to the contrary, ultimately in support of the hero.

Sometimes the hero has to win over the father and convince him that he is someone worthy of being helped. In these cases, the father will not help someone who has not been thoroughly tested and proved through hardship and pain. Everything that went before, crossing the first threshold and overcoming the road of trials and fending off temptation, was designed to prepare the hero for this moment.

To stand before your creator to be evaluated *in toto* is a sobering thing. The mother's gaze is likely to be much more tolerant and forgiving. But the father, the powerful force of male energy that lives not with the women and children but embodies the vigor of the village—the very fate-holder of the tribe—can respect only strength, valor, and endurance.

If the hero is to become a man, it is his father who must perform the initiation. Only the father can bestow on the son the mark of manhood.

But atonement with the father is also about what the son sees in the father. In facing his father, the hero must, in Campbell's words, "open his soul beyond terror to such a degree that he will ... understand how the ... tragedies of this vast and ruthless cosmos are completely validated. ... The hero transcends life ... and for a moment rises to a glimpse of the source. He beholds the face of the father, understands—and the two are atoned."

The son must make peace with the father and come to understand and accept that there is reason and meaning behind the madness of life. It's the acceptance and unification of all the strange and disparate parts of what it means to be alive.

This is the hero's moment of enlightenment. After he has this encounter with the father, he stops wondering why he suffers. He starts seeing meaning behind even his own hardships, and things that were seen as negative are suddenly revealed to have been what allowed him to have success. No more does he wonder what's happening to him. Now he understands.

Often, atonement in the father involves the hero's death, at least in some sense. It's the death of the child so the man can be born. Many stories involve a death and rebirth.

Now the hero, no longer a child, and no longer a victim tossed about by the waves, has become a doer, an agent of change, a powerful player in the game of life. He takes responsibility. He stops complaining. He no longer looks to be helped but to help. He is now a man.

Luke Skywalker beholds the true face of his father. His father tells him he is proud of him, and the son forgives the father. In *Finding Nemo,* Nemo and his father, Marlin, reconcile after being separated for the whole movie (and after both undergo hero's journeys). In a metaphorical sense, Mulan has her meeting with the father when it is revealed that she is a woman and is abandoned by her former friends. In this moment of truth, she determines to gird her loins (so to speak) and do the right thing.

This is the gut-check, the pivotal moment, the sink-or-swim time. There may or may not be an actual father or even a father figure involved, but after this event the hero no longer vacillates about what to do. It all becomes clear, and now all that is left is to carry it out.

Apostasis

Apostasis is a fancy word that means to become divine.

Now that the hero has met with the father and become a man, he steps into his superpowers. This is a state of ascended knowledge, power, and peace that has come as a result of the rite of passage the hero has been on. Sometimes it comes after dying and being reborn.

When Neo (in *The Matrix*) is killed by the Agents, he comes back to life and suddenly has enlightenment. He is master of the Matrix now, and the Agents—the villains of the film—turn and run from him in terror.

When King Théoden (in *The Return of the King*) faces his own cowardice and masters it, he rests in absolute peace, though he is dying. He has defeated his demons and won enlightenment, a solace, as his prize.

After Luke has faced the revelation of who is father really is, and lost a limb in the process, he achieves understanding. When we see him next, he is a Jedi in full command of his powers.

As a result of this transformative journey, the hero is now more than he was. He is more than his mother, more than his father. He has encompassed the gentleness that wins the goddess and the perseverance that convinces the destroyer-father, and now he is something larger than either one.

These new powers and insights, these new plateaus of understanding and might, are the benefits the hero now has to offer the village and the tribe. Now he can really contribute to the salvation of his people. He is now master and commander, a man in full.

The Ultimate Boon

This is when the good guys win. The hero achieves the victory he's been trying to get for the full journey.

The Ring of Power is cast into the Cracks of Doom, and Middle-earth is saved. The proton torpedo goes into the shaft, and the Death Star is destroyed. Simba (in *The Lion King*) strides up Pride

Rock and roars, signifying the return of the rightful king. Harry Potter faces off against Lord Voldemort one last time, and He Who Shall Not Be Named is finally destroyed.

If the atonement with the father is said to be the moment of truth in the hero's inner journey, then the ultimate boon is the climax of the external plot. Now that the hero has stepped into his powers as a man, he can finally achieve the impossible task.

Refusal of the Return

Once the hero has achieved so much in the great and wondrous world beyond the village, he may not feel like going back there. Back there, people may still think of him as a child. Back there, there is no goddess or mystical marriage. Back there, chores await and everything is mundane.

What's more, in the new world, he has carved out a place for himself. He has friends and allies and possibly a host of people who are grateful to him. "There's a place for you here," they say. "Won't you stay and make a life with us?"

In *The Lion King,* Simba has become a grown lion out in the jungle, away from his family. Eventually, family life finds him, and he is urged to come back and set things to rights in his home. But he refuses. His new approach to life is one in which he doesn't try to fix things. Something must convince him to do what is right.

In *The Dark Knight Rises,* Bruce Wayne does not rejoin the people of Gotham City after defeating his enemies in the previous film. He is a recluse hiding in his mansion, feeling that the people don't need him now. But of course they do.

In *Saving Private Ryan,* the heroes have overcome overwhelming odds during the D-Day invasion and beyond to locate Private Ryan so he can be pulled from combat and sent home. He is the last of several brothers, the rest of whom have recently died in the war. A great battle is impending, and Private Ryan has no intention of leaving his comrades to face that without him. He refuses to return home.

Most heroes in fiction and film do not refuse or even hesitate to begin journeying back home, but you can see why they might. Still, a hero's journey story is not complete until he has reintegrated into the tribe, but now as an adult. Learning the secrets and achieving his powers and then spending those on others besides his home village is like a boy who went into the jungle for his rite of passage but found such a nice spot in the shade that he never came home. It's an incomplete journey, a there-but-not-back-again, that will probably anger your reader's brain, so I encourage you to let him make the final trek homeward.

Magic Flight

There is a sense in which the hero's journey is a heist caper. A mere human has entered into the realm of the gods, laid his hands upon some divine item, and is trying to get back into the human world with it.

Get him!

In myth, sometimes the hero has done exactly that. Jack goes up the beanstalk and steals a variety of things, including a goose that lays golden eggs. But then the giant gets wind of him, and Jack must make a hasty escape.

In film and fiction, sometimes the hero has to get away quick, too, even though the main action of the story has been resolved. Luke and his fellow survivors had better get away from the Death Star before it blows. Indiana Jones and his father and friends (in *Indiana Jones and the Last Crusade*) have wisely left the Holy Grail behind, but now they'd better get out of the hidden chamber before the cavern collapses and traps them inside forever.

Rescue from Without

Sometimes the hero needs help to escape.

Frodo and Sam have cast the Ring into the Cracks of Doom, but it takes giant eagles to save them from the erupting volcano.

Dorothy has defeated the Wicked Witch of the West, but she needs a magical hot air balloon to carry her home.

Even if the hero isn't making a run for it, there still has to be a whisking away from the world of the initiation and a return to the homelands. It might be a jump into hyperspace or a ride on a Pegasus or a flight on a 777, but a great distance (even if only metaphorical) must be crossed to bring the hero home.

This isn't the same as a *deus ex machina*, where a divine figure comes in and sets everything right, thus depriving the hero of the opportunity to learn his lesson and make the change himself.

Crossing the Return Threshold

Now comes the challenge of integrating what the hero has learned on his journey into what he knows of life back at home. Now that he has become a man, almost a superman, how can that be used to benefit the tribe?

Readers sometimes wonder why The Lord of the Rings trilogy ends with such a prolonged section. After the Ring is destroyed and Aragorn is installed as king, what more is left to be done, storywise?

But Tolkien was writing not just an adventure tale but a hero's journey, and that story is not complete until the hero can bring what he has learned and achieved and *become* during his initiation back to help his people.

This is sometimes called the "return with the elixir," because it implies that he's found something on his trek that he needs to bring back to restore the health of his home village.

In Tolkien's novel *The Return of the King* (but not in the film version), when Frodo and his companions return to their beloved Shire, they find the place in chaos. Some new powerful human (Sharkey) has moved in and turned their home into a police state. The local hobbits don't know what to do. They're leaderless and weak, like the sheep of their beloved hills.

It is Frodo's moment. Yes, he saved the world, but when it comes right down to it, saving the Shire is an even bigger challenge. No army of tall human allies or wizards or flying eagles to come to his aid now. Frodo and the friends who went with him on the journey rally the people and defeat Sharkey and his gang, sending them packing and saving their home.

The chapter is called "The Scouring of the Shire," and it is Frodo's way of bringing back to his family, to his village, the heroism he has learned on his journey. The Frodo at the beginning of the tale would've cowered in the corner with the others if faced with such enemies. But the Frodo at the end of his journey is a hero of legend.

Not everyone will listen to the hero upon his return. Not everyone will accept his leadership or his nuggets of wisdom. The language of the mystical world of his adventure may not translate well to the mundane world of those who have not been there. So the hero is content to teach those who will listen and rise to the challenge when the need for his skills arises.

Master of Two Worlds

Just because the hero has returned to the mundane world doesn't mean he no longer visits that outer world that seems so strange to his fellows.

Sam Gamgee may have returned with Frodo from the great adventure, and Frodo may be gone, but Sam's life is not all gardens and babies now. He might also be caught wandering beyond the fringes of the Shire and consorting with the likes of wizards, elves, and dwarves. Neo has power over the Agents in the Matrix, and he can go in and out of that world at will, and this is exactly what he does to continue the effort to deliver mankind.

The hero will no longer be entirely at home in the mundane world. He is like Disney's Tarzan, who can communicate with both humans and animals. He could find an abode in either world, but he needs to venture into both worlds to feel complete.

Part of the great awakening the hero experiences on his journey is the realization that the mundane world and the supernatural world beyond it are one and the same. They are interconnected.

They overlay one another. He never really left that ordinary world, but then, he's not entirely back from that supernatural world either. He is master of both worlds now, able to pluck fruit from either one to make a salad in the other. Symbols are reality, and realities are only symbolic.

Disney's *The Incredibles* features a family of superheroes. For years, they had to hide their powers and their identities. But through the crucible of a great adventure, they earned the right to don their superhero attire whenever the need arises. Sometimes they're going to school and doing dishes, and sometimes they're schooling supervillains and dishing out justice. They belong in both worlds. They are powerful in both. They have fun in both. They are free to live.

Freedom to Live

As the hero rests in the confidence born of his journey and insights and new mastery, he can live without fear. He doesn't fear death, because he has faced it. He doesn't fear danger, because he has overcome it. He doesn't fear enemies, because he has vanquished them. He no longer has to live in anxiety about the future, and he can live fully in the moment, knowing that he will have an answer to whatever comes.

Not only is the hero now a man of the tribe, in a sense he is an elder and a shaman, even if he is still young. Compare his state before the journey—safe, protected, but naive, whiny, and immature—with this powerful master of two worlds.

At the end of the hero's journey story you write, your hero will be in a special state of confidence and bliss, able to handle all situations with panache and skill—or at least the situations that once vexed him. Here at the end, he will experience all the rewards of manhood—leadership, veneration, confidence, and perhaps the affections of a certain goddess. He has faced the unknown and overcome it. He has realized that he is strong, and he has put the things of childhood behind him. And now he can face the future without fear.

CONCLUSION

The hero's journey is useful as a road map for a multitude of transformation stories. They are inevitably full of conflict (struggle), and they're about someone going through something that nearly every reader can relate to, so they're strong candidates for stories that will please your reader.

There is something so powerful about the hero's journey. I remember being a twelve-year-old sitting in a theater in Phoenix in the summer of 1977 (yes, do the math), watching George Lucas's masterpiece, the original *Star Wars*, and feeling as if the top of my skull had been removed so that this story could be plugged directly into my cerebral cortex. Never had a story impacted me so utterly. It was perfect, almost like a dream.

It's no accident that Lucas got the hero's journey so perfectly right for his movie: He had Joseph Campbell help him with the script!

Some have called the hero's journey sequence nothing more than a simple "fish out of water" story, where someone is put into a context he's not familiar with and has to learn the new rules. Well, it certainly is that, but I feel it will serve your stories better—perhaps energize them more fully—if you write them with a more serious eye toward Campbell's seventeen stages.

If you're looking for a story structure that will be certain to engage your reader's brain in a powerful and positive way, you will find few better than the hero's journey.

Chapter 26
ARCHETYPES

Our second stop on the brain's greatest hits world tour is Jung's archetypes.

Around the beginning of the twentieth century, Swiss psychiatrist Carl Gustav Jung developed the idea of "archaic remnants" or "primordial images" that reside in every person's psyche. He likened these to mythological images or motifs, and he felt these common ideas about "types" (hence arche*types*) of people were so vital to humans that they were essentially psychological organs, just as necessary as physical organs.

Examples of archetypes include the mother, the mentor, the jester, the mystic, and the king. They are *roles* that people around us play. Archetypes are slippery and flexible, and we all play multiple archetypal roles at various times in our lives and even at different moments in the day. We might be father in the morning, king during the workday, friend after work, and then gladiator on the highway going home.

I referred to several sources as I wrote this chapter. One of them was Jeannie Campbell's *Character Therapist* blog series on archetypes. You may also find *45 Master Characters* by Victoria Lynn Schmidt useful.

The nice thing about archetypes for the fiction writer is that these people types are already residing in your reader's brain. You don't have to devote a lot of energy to explaining what the maiden character is or why the abuser is abusive—your reader already knows those people. It's a form of shorthand, if you will.

Now, we can and should make our archetypal characters interesting and nuanced. We want archetypes, not stereotypes. We want to show the reader that this person is behaving like the seductress or the recluse, filling that role (at least for right now), but we don't need to paint that character as the quintessential seductress or the pure recluse. Layered characters are usually better than stock characters. So try not to use these character types as the culmination of your characters' personalities. Go deeper.

But archetypes are a nice tool to cause your characters to register deep within your reader's brain, keeping her engaged with your book.

JUNG'S TWELVE ARCHETYPES

Jung recognized many sorts of archetypes. Some say there are sixty or more. The book I referred to earlier lists forty-five. Jung acknowledged the many but kept his list to twelve.

Jung also realized that there is a shadowy flipside to each of his twelve archetypes, a bad counterpart to every good type.

The Innocent

The good aspect of this type is the person who is a child at heart. This is Cinderella and Forrest Gump and Dorothy (in *The Wizard of Oz*) and WALL-E.

The innocent is friendly and naive, happy and simple, virtuous and wholesome and honest. This person is lighthearted and loyal, playful and delightful to be around. There may be a magical aspect to the innocent, possibly arising from her innocence.

The bad aspect of the innocent is that he may be too foolish or childish, thus endangering others or shirking responsibility. The innocent may be overly gullible or dependent or so simplistic and naive that negative outcomes result.

As with every archetype, the innocent can shift from the good aspect to the bad in a heartbeat. In the movie version of *The Fellowship of the Ring*, Pippin—a childlike innocent if ever there was one—has had his tongue so loosened by ale that he nearly reveals Frodo's identity to a crowd of cruel strangers trying to capture Frodo. He was having fun and partying in the moment, and any thought of restraining his words had vanished. As the wizard Gandalf later says: Pippin is a fool, but an honest fool.

The Orphan or Everyman/Everywoman

This archetype is the "they" in "That's what they say." This is the regular guy or typical woman. The working stiff, the good citizen, the silent majority, the Walmart shopper.

The connection between the orphan and a regular Jane is that this person had to learn the pragmatic realities of life at an early age. This doesn't mean she is an orphan in any technical sense. It's just that she's a realist. She's not so concerned with philosophy or politics or the state of the human heart but with where dinner is coming from. This makes her both independent and interdependent. She has few pretenses and tends to be empathetic.

Almost every character Jimmy Stewart played in movies is this character. He's unassuming and genuine and believes the best in everyone. The orphan type has a dogged resilience and is a good networker.

The bad aspect of the orphan/everywoman is when she can blame others for her problems or play the victim card. She can also become a sullen loner, feeling that everything is against her. Her desire to belong is so strong that she can end up getting into abusive relationships and staying in them long term.

The orphan can flip-flop from good to bad and back again pretty quickly. So we see both aspects in orphan/everyman characters like Frodo Baggins, Batman, Spider-Man, and many other superhero characters. The straight orphan type is exemplified in characters like Little Orphan Annie, Harry Potter, Tarzan, Luke Skywalker, Mowgli (in *The Jungle Book*), and George Bailey (Jimmy Stewart's character in *It's a Wonderful Life* is the poster child for this archetype).

The Hero

The hero, also called the warrior, is your crusader, your (nonbrooding) superhero, your dragon slayer, your champion, and your valiant soldier.

The hero is nothing if not courageous. In fact, courage may be this archetype's greatest attribute. He or she wants only to win, to conquer, to prevail. The hero's enemies may be of the mind as much as upon a field of battle or in a corporate conference room. This is Mulan and Rocky, Neo and Buffy, James Bond and Robin Hood and Flick (in *A Bug's Life*).

The hero is a tough cookie, both physically and mentally. He is protective and athletic, assertive and tenacious. You won't find a more noble companion or a more confident champion of the underdog. Ripley in *Alien* and especially *Aliens* is an amazing hero character.

The hero's negative aspect is that he can become ruthless and cruel. He can be manipulative and impulsive, rushing into action without considering the consequences. He might, like Marty McFly in *Back to the Future*, foolishly accept any challenge to prove he's not a chicken. His heroism can be poisoned, as when winsome Anakin Skywalker becomes the dreaded villain Darth Vader.

We all love our heroes, and your novel would do well with one or more of them. Remember to make them layered and realistic, using my system in *Plot Versus Character* or however you create believable characters for fiction. Go beyond the stereotype and even the archetype, until you've depicted a real person performing the role of hero because of her innate drive to be courageous and protective.

The Caregiver

Ah, the saint. The altruistic helper who wants only to care for others. We all know one or more of these angels of mercy, even if it's something we glimpse only now and then. We feel this impulse ourselves at times, although who and what we feel compassion toward may be different from others or shift over time. Still, we know what it feels like to want to nurture.

The caregiver is Mother Teresa and Florence Nightingale. It's Oskar Schindler and Atticus Finch (from *To Kill a Mockingbird*). It's Renee Zellweger's characters in *Jerry Maguire* and *Shark Tale.* It's Maria in *The Sound of Music* and Dumbo's mother in *Dumbo.* It's Earth Mother and Big Mama and dear ol' Santa.

Doctors and nurses are often caregivers, as are pastors and priests, therapists and aid workers and customer service managers—anyone who wants to turn his love of helping people into an occupation. They find meaning and fulfillment in caring for others.

The caregiver can be taken advantage of, which plays on his fear of being overlooked and unappreciated. On the dark side, the caregiver can play the martyr, can be smothering and overprotective, and can motivate others through guilt. They can have trouble saying "no," leading to feelings of resentment. They can run themselves down and become the selfish sort of person they loathe. Trying to please everyone may make them seem like they have no spine. And of course, a caregiver can become the cat lady.

But in the end, the caregiver will sacrifice himself for the good of others, and your reader's brain *digs* people like that.

The Explorer

The explorer, also called the seeker, wants to know what's *out there.* So Amelia Earhart straps on her goggles and heads into the blue, Captain Kirk sits in the captain's chair and boldly goes where no one has gone before, Indiana Jones grabs his whip and plunges into the tunnel, and Jacques Cousteau dons his scuba tank and goes looking around underwater.

These people are often heroes in our definition, but in Jungian terms they are not heroes but explorers, because the plumbing of unknown realms is their primary motivation.

Some people just want to be like Winnie the Pooh and "go on an explore." They're spelunkers and pioneers and mountain climbers.

They want to see the world from space or the inside of an atom or the shape of the continents. They are Lewis and Clark, Ferdinand Magellan, and Leif Ericson, even if only figuratively speaking.

The explorer fears being fenced in, so she leaves the known world behind and strikes out on her own. That could be expressed in entrepreneurism as easily as interstellar mapping. Freedom is what she wants. She seeks autonomy, excitement, and the new. She bores easily and fears getting pinned down, so you can expect her to up and leave without notice, whether that's a departure from a house or a relationship.

On the down side, the explorer can become a nonconformist just for the sake of nonconforming, more like an intentional misfit than an actually unique individual. The unwillingness to settle down will make her miss the treasures that would come if she did. She may be so bent on doing it herself that she is unable to accomplish goals that could easily be achieved in concert with others. Always seeking the new thing out there may cause her to overlook the great thing she has right here.

Still, if you need a wilderness explored or a new sort of business model pioneered or a new land settled, the explorer is your archetype.

The Rebel

The rebel is a wild man, the fiery revolutionary whose outrageous efforts for radical freedom could bring down the whole system he sets his sights upon, for good or ill.

If an authority is corrupt, it needs to be overhauled—and if it can't be overhauled, it must be overthrown. Rebels know this. They gravitate to what they perceive as oppressive regimes and begin chopping away at the trunk.

Rebels are dangerous, even if they're on our side. They don't really have a place in a civil society. If things are settled and egalitarian, the rebel is bored. To feel powerful and effective, he must seek out injustice and begin the revolution all over again.

In the world of business, the rebel can be counted on to perceive what processes aren't working and lead the charge to bring about change. Rebels are unconventional thinkers, which makes them innovative and original.

They're not usually among the leadership's star pupils. Like Maverick in *Top Gun*, rebels buck authority just on principle. They're not exactly respecters of office or rank.

It's not hard to see how the rebel can perceive pretty much everything as being unfair, thus giving him the justification he needs to turn criminal. Ah, wealth has been distributed unequally, so I should take some of it from someone else to make things more even. Ah, it's not fair that this person should have that car, so I think I should have it for myself. The rebel can turn into a rogue as quick as a snap.

Rebels gone bad often carry violence and the threat of violence as an overt part of their persona. In *Star Wars: The Phantom Menace*, the young Obi-Wan Kenobi and Darth Maul are essentially mirror images of one another. What makes Darth Maul a rebel, in Jungian terms, is that he would just as soon slice you up as talk to you.

Good rebels are Zorro, Henry Ford, Robin Hood, Madame Curie, Han Solo, Martin Luther, George Orwell, Malcolm Reynolds (in *Firefly*), Rosa Parks, and Thomas Jefferson. Rebels turned into bad boys or girls include Jim Stark (James Dean's character in *Rebel Without a Cause*), Al Capone, both James and Caius (in the *Twilight* movies), Madonna, Bender (in *The Breakfast Club*), and Aphrodite, who was punished by Zeus for seducing her fellow gods.

The Lover

The lover is the idealist, the starry-eyed Romeo gazing across the courtyard to see what light from yonder window breaks. The lover is also the Don Juan, seeking love (or just sex) as an end in and of itself. The lover can be the hopeless romantic projecting perfection on yet another person she's just met.

The lover is the intimate, the team player, the helpmeet, the partner, the enthusiast, and the spouse. She is passionate, committed, and a great giver of appreciation. This may be the encourager or the sex symbol or the reader of romance novels. She is the pursuer of pure ideals, the chief of which is true love.

This is Rick (Humphrey Bogart's character in *Casablanca*), Rose (Kate Winslet's character in *Titanic*), Buttercup and Westley (in *The Princess Bride*), Tony and Maria (in *West Side Story*), and Jay Gatsby.

The lover is intense and emotional, but where she really shines is when feeling infatuated, causing infatuation (flirting, seducing), and falling helplessly in love. She spends much of her energy imagining, engendering, keeping, and recapturing the love of others.

The bad aspect of the lover is the woman (or man) scorned. The lover can be vindictive, addicted, promiscuous, jealous, and, like the female black widow, carnivorous (metaphorically speaking, we hope). The lover gone bad can become a Delilah or a Casanova or an Alex Forrest (Glenn Close's murderous character in *Fatal Attraction*).

Many of us become jaded as we mature, losing some of that dreamy belief in humanitarian ideals like justice, compassion, and the value of helping a lost puppy. The lover reminds us what it felt like to gaze with wonder at a dewdrop or give with generosity or dance without caring who sees.

The Creator

If you can imagine it, it can be done—that's the motto of the creator. This is the artist and the architect, the composer and the choreographer, the writer and the actor. The creator longs to create things of enduring value, and to that end he develops his creative abilities.

The creator might be a performer, like a musician or dancer, but he is more likely to be the person *creating* the thing being performed. He is the inventor, the visionary, the innovator, and the dreamer.

There is a sense in which the creator is on a lifelong journey of discovery—trying to discover himself. What is it I really feel? Who is it I really want to be? How is it I really want to live? The things he creates along this quest are his efforts at articulating, or at least exploring, answers to those questions.

This is Walt Disney and Mozart and Christian (Ewan McGregor's character in *Moulin Rouge!*) and John Denver and Michael Jackson. This is the creator goddess and Mother Nature and Jo March (Winona Ryder's character in *Little Women*).

Like rebels, creators are innovative thinkers. They have an uncanny ability—and need—to express themselves. Whether it's poetry or photography or some clever invention, they're always trying to take what's in their mind and make it observable for others, sometimes to say something important, sometimes just to get it out of their head.

The dark side of creators is when they try to play god. Their innovations are not to express themselves but to force people to change. A pursuit of excellence in their craft can become the cruelest of taskmasters, even driving them insane, as we saw so elegantly portrayed in *Amadeus*.

What a creator doesn't want is to be mediocre in his vision or craft. His creations may end up with little sense or meaning, but they will be as technically brilliant as he can make them. So he challenges himself to be audacious and daring, but also as skilled as he can be.

The Jester

Enter the trickster, the comedian whose greatest fear is to be bored—or boring to others. She's the jokester, the fool, and the party animal.

It has been said that the goal of the fool, to fully enjoy life as she finds it, may make her the wisest of us all. She must be alive and present in the moment. Thinking too much about yesterday or tomorrow that today gets away would be a serious sin.

It's a remarkable phenomenon that the court jester can get away with saying things to the king that would get anyone else guillotined. Same with puppets and animated characters. And the goofier or more out of touch the jester is, the more outrageous (and insightful) things she's able to say.

Pretty much any movie starring Eddie Murphy, Chevy Chase, Chris Tucker, Ben Stiller, or Adam Sandler is going to feature the jester character. And they're in good company, as Odysseus (hero of Homer's *Odyssey* and *Iliad*) was a trickster character, too, often using humor or his wits to get out of tight spots and suggest the occasional Trojan Horse, which is itself a sick sort of joke.

Trickster characters often set the whole story in motion: Puck (in Shakespeare's *A Midsummer Night's Dream*), Jack Sparrow (in *Pirates of the Caribbean*), Bugs Bunny, and Q in *Star Trek: The Next Generation,* for example.

Usually, jester characters are male, but stage plays like *She Stoops to Conquer, Twelfth Night, As You Like It,* and *Two Gentlemen of Verona*—along with, not coincidentally, the movie *Shakespeare in Love*—feature female tricksters.

Jesters can be innocent and well meaning, like Gilligan or Buddy (Will Ferrell's character in *Elf*) or Dory (in *Finding Nemo*), or they can be darker, like Jim Carrey as the Grinch or as Fletcher Reede (in *Liar Liar*).

Jesters are useful characters for fiction, even if it's just the protagonist's funny friend (like Lenny, Steve Zahn's character in *That Thing You Do!,* or Phoebe, Lisa Kudrow's character in *Friends*). The brain needs breaks and breathers, you'll recall, and comic relief is a great way to give that to your reader.

The Sage

"Help me, Obi-Wan Kenobi. You're my only hope."

Here is the mentor, the expert, the philosopher, the Zen (or Jedi) master. Here is Gandalf and Merlin and Dumbledore and Mr. Spock. Here is the Oracle in *The Matrix* and Yoda in *The Empire Strikes Back.* Here is Oprah Winfrey and Dr. Phil and Gandhi.

A sage can be a scholar, a detective, an advisor, a professor, or nearly any sort of doctor. The sage offers wisdom, insight, intelligence, analysis, and synthesis, all of which can be hugely valuable to your other characters.

Most often, the sage is a resource to be consulted by the hero, like the mystical master sitting atop a proverbial mountaintop, to be approached whenever someone doesn't know what to do next. In the television series *Merlin,* for instance, it is The Dragon (voiced by John Hurt) to whom the adolescent Merlin goes for counsel. Less often, the sage is himself or herself the protagonist, like Sherlock Holmes or Mary Poppins.

Sages are introspective and investigative. They see patterns where others do not. They have thus achieved a level of understanding that is the envy of others. Their minds are on philosophies and first causes and the meaning of world events. They see through the smoke to what's really going on.

Turned to the bad side, the sage can become, as the saying goes, "so heavenly minded that he's of no earthly good," sitting in his ivory tower thinking lofty thoughts about Keats and Milton. He can begin to think of regular people as lesser beings, as does Henry Higgins in *My Fair Lady.*

The sage hates to be duped or at a loss for what to do. He much prefers to be the one doling out advice, not having to seek it. As such, the sage can develop a pride that may prevent him from obtaining the help he needs. Humility is not always high on the list of the sage's attributes.

Still, when you need to level up in your understanding, who you really want is a sage.

The Magician

The magician is the master of secret knowledge. She has bent these forces to her will so fully that she can unleash them to terrifying or amazing effect on the world.

It may not be magic, per se. As novelist Arthur C. Clarke famously said, "Any sufficiently advanced technology is indistinguishable from magic." So the magician may be, like the so-called Wizard of Oz, merely a technician.

What's important is the mastery.

The magician is also the wizard, the warlock, the witch, the high priest, the shaman, the healer, the sorcerer, and the medicine man. She understands the fundamental laws of the universe (or of technology) and she uses those to make dreams come true.

Magicians are all about bringing visions to life. They harness the most powerful forces available to them to evoke change and forge solutions. Their goal isn't to do magic tricks but to truly *transform* things, including people. Including, perhaps, themselves.

They enjoy seeming mysterious, like the stereotypical tarot card reader conducting a séance.

If a magician turns bad, it can be disastrous for everyone around her. Indeed, nearly every fantasy film or fairy tale has a dark magician as its villain. Consider Maleficent (in the movie by that name and also in *Sleeping Beauty*) and Lord Voldemort and Queen Narissa (Susan Sarandon's character in *Enchanted*) and Darth Vader and Ursula (in *The Little Mermaid*) and both Sauron and Saruman (in *The Lord of the Rings*) and Loki (in *Thor*).

It is a terrifying thing when the fundamental forces of the universe are turned against the good people of the world. That's true in everyday life as much as in science fiction and fantasy.

The Ruler

At last, the return of the king! How like God is the archetype of the good king. He seems to be all-knowing and all-powerful, full of justice and wisdom. He is mighty in battle and merciful in his dealings. His mind is on the welfare of his people, and enemies would do well to tremble at the tramp of his boot. Rulers like King Arthur and Aragorn (in *The Lord of the Rings*) and even Queen Elizabeth seem larger than life, superhuman.

The ruler is commander, general, empress, president, CEO. He is the one who gives leadership and establishes the rules and sets the tone for the whole organization, army, or realm. He carries many responsibilities and has to spend much of his time administrating, hearing reports, and doling out justice.

A ruler aspires to influence how things are done and how people go about their affairs. He may also crave power and wealth, but mostly he desires to create a successful and prosperous community, business, family, and/or kingdom.

The ruler wants things to go "just so." So long as someone else is in charge, that may not be the case. The solution, then, is to not work for anyone else but to be the boss.

If the ruler turns bad, he can become a tyrant, a despot, and a monster—maybe a godfather. Rulers can become corrupted, and they can come to fear being overthrown so much that they behave like King Herod and murder everyone, even children, who might become a rival. A king turned evil is a terrifying person to meet.

OTHER ARCHETYPES, STEREOTYPES, AND STOCK CHARACTERS

All right, so now you've heard Jung's twelve main archetypes. I think they're powerful symbols that will be effective for you in your own fiction, as they spark something in the reader's brain and cause her to pay attention.

But there are many other people "types" that can be used in your fiction. Below I offer a sampling of them just to see if the terms trigger something in your mind as you think about your story. A simple Google search will lead you to more information about the ones that strike your fancy.

- The outcast/scapegoat
- The battle-axe
- The reluctant hero
- The town drunk
- The tortured artist
- The backstabber
- The punisher
- The nemesis/shadow self
- The group of companions
- The loyal retainer (like Batman's protégé, Robin)
- The unfaithful wife
- The damsel in distress
- The mad scientist
- The absent-minded professor

- The evil clown
- The fop
- The gentle giant
- The rival
- The psychic
- The derelict
- The temptress
- The creature of nightmare
- The bimbo
- The dumb blonde
- The abuser
- The recluse
- The blind seer
- The Jewish mother
- The Latin lover
- The jock
- The Mary Sue
- The mama's boy
- The female messiah
- The lost soul
- The Gorgon
- The Amazon
- The ingénue
- The hotshot
- The hooker with a heart of gold
- The shrew
- The supersoldier
- The town bully
- The tomboy
- The yokel or barfly
- The hypocritical priest
- The nerd
- The noble savage
- The hag or crone
- The femme fatale

I could go on and on, but I think you get the idea. Your reader's mind is fairly overpopulated with characters he knows—or has learned—and will readily identify them when they show up in your fiction.

I'm not advocating stereotypes, as I've mentioned before. You can use the power of archetypes without lapsing into stereotype, but you have to be conscious of the effort. An old man might be a good mentor character for your book, but what if the role of mentor in your story were played by someone or something unexpected, like a robot or a cricket or a little girl? Someone can be an explorer archetype without being Ponce de Leon, after all. Tap into the psychological strength of these character types without surrendering to shallow caricature.

Chapter 27
ARISTOTLE'S *RHETORIC*

Our final stop on the brain's greatest hits world tour is an ancient book written by the philosopher Aristotle—student of Plato, teacher of Alexander the Great, and arguably the first genuine scientist in history. Aristotle applied his towering intellect to topics as far ranging as physics and biology, logic and poetry, politics and metaphysics.

He also studied rhetoric, the art of using speech to persuade, influence, or please the hearer. In other words, he made it the focus of his scientific inquiry to figure out how to use words to engage someone.

If he were alive and studying this today, we might call him a narratologist or a neuroscientist, and he'd no doubt be putting electrodes on his volunteers to measure their brain activity as they watched movies, read novels, and listened to speeches. He wanted to know how the words could be delivered so that the recipient experienced the emotions the word-giver intended.

I'd say his findings might be of interest to the novelist. We want our reader to keep reading our fiction to the end (and maybe to tell others about how great our novel is!). And we want our reader to *feel* an array of things: empathy for our hero, anger at our villain, indignation at some injustice in the story, or whatever else.

Earlier, Dr. Zak had us thinking about hacking the reader's brain. Now, we're hacking the reader's emotions. And you thought this was a book about fiction.

THE THREE MEANS OF PERSUASION

In his writings on the subject, Aristotle seemed to have in mind a speaker addressing a crowd or, more specifically, one or more *judges* who must make a decision after hearing perhaps one speaker in favor of some proposal and one speaker opposed. It was imperative, then, that the word-spinner be able to move his audience in the direction he desired. He discovered three primary ways to persuade someone. You persuade through the character of the speaker, the emotional state of the hearer, or the argument itself.

Method #1: A speaker will persuade his audience if he seems credible.

Methods one and three will be of lesser interest to us, so I'll give the briefest of overviews. Persuasion-by-character is accomplished "whenever the speech is held in such a way as to render the speaker worthy of credence. If the speaker appears to be credible, the audience will [believe] that propositions put forward by the credible speaker are true or acceptable." In other words, if you sound like you know what you're talking about, the hearer will be inclined to believe whatever you say.

How? He must display all three of these: "(i) practical intelligence (*phronêsis*), (ii) a virtuous character, and (iii) good will." And, "it must be stressed that the speaker must accomplish these effects by *what* he says; it is not necessary that he is actually virtuous, etc." This is likely more pertinent for writers of nonfiction than fiction. So let's move ahead.

Method #2: A speaker will persuade his audience if he puts them in the right mood.

The success of the speech (or novel), Aristotle said, "depends on the emotional dispositions of the audience; for we do not judge in the same way when we grieve [as when we] rejoice or when we are friendly [as when we are] hostile. Thus, the orator has to arouse emotions exactly because emotions have the power to modify our judgments."

How? The trick is to target what emotion you want your reader to feel and then to consciously do what it takes to arouse that emotion. "With this equipment, the orator will be able, for example, to highlight such characteristics of a case as are likely to provoke anger in the audience."

We'll return to this in a moment.

Method #3: A speaker will persuade his audience if he makes a great case.

This is the power of the courtroom attorney making such a rousing speech and presenting such conclusive evidence that the judge and jury can't help but conclude that what she says is in fact true. From Aristotle: "We persuade by the argument itself when we demonstrate or seem to demonstrate that something is the case."

ARISTOTLE IS HACKING YOUR EMOTIONS

Ten chapters of Book II of Aristotle's *Rhetoric* are devoted to defining the various emotions an audience (or reader) might have and spelling out exactly how to rouse those emotions.

My objective in presenting these is to enable you to persuade your reader to do one thing and one thing only: engage with your book. Our chief commandment is to keep the reader engaged from beginning to end, and dear ol' Uncle Aristotle is going to give us some time-honored strategies for doing so.

Also consider how you might use these to make your reader feel various emotions at different points throughout the story. You may want her to feel elated at one point and disgusted at another and relaxed at a third. That's a great way to think about your scenes, so I hope you'll use this to help you. But my main goal is for you to get your reader hooked and keep her on the hook.

We won't be looking at all the emotions Aristotle examines. For instance, he talks about making the hearer/reader feel shame, and I personally don't see any need for the writer of fiction to try to make a reader feel that way. If you'd like to explore Aristotle's other chapters on emotions and persuasion, I encourage you to do so on your own.

Friendliness

The main way to engage your reader is to make her feel connected to your hero. If she feels like this is a person she would like—or who is *like* her—she will engage with your book. We want, in short, to make your reader feel *friendly* toward your protagonist, to feel that this is someone with whom she could be friends.

To that end, we can examine Aristotle's work on engendering feelings of friendliness in the listener or reader.

"We may [define having] friendly feeling towards any one as [when you] wish for him what you believe to be good things," Aristotle says. "Not for your own sake but for his, and being inclined, so far as you can, to bring these things about." He's defining friendship here. He says it's when you hope the other person has good things happen to him. We want your reader rooting for the home team.

One way to make the reader feel friendship toward your protagonist is to show him treating with kindness the sort of person we ourselves would care about. "We feel friendly to those who have treated us well, either ourselves or those we care for," Aristotle says, "whether on a large scale, or readily, or at some particular crisis; provided it was for [the] sake of someone besides the doer."

In other words, this is a nice person who helps others just because they need help. Show us your hero doing that, and we'll begin to like him. (It follows that, to make us *dislike* someone, you ought to show him mistreating someone we care for.)

Another way to make us feel friendly toward your hero is to show him opposing those whom we ourselves would oppose. "And also to those who are enemies to those whose enemies we are, and dislike, or are disliked by, those whom we dislike. For all such persons think the things good which we think good, so that they wish what is good for us; and this ... is what friends ... do." If your reader would stand up to a bully, show your hero standing up to a bully, and your reader will love your hero.

Aristotle says we also like "those who are willing to treat us well where money or our personal safety is concerned: and therefore we value those who are [generous], brave, or just." Show your hero being generous, brave, or just, and your reader will love her.

Aristotle listed several categories of people we like. Make your hero one or more of these, especially near the beginning of the story, and we'll connect with him. We like:

- **THE CHARMING OR ADMIRABLE:** "And also those whose friends we wish to be, if it is plain that they wish to be our friends: such are the morally good, and those well thought of by every one, by the best men, or by those whom we admire or who admire us."
- **THE NICE AND PLEASANT:** "And also those with whom it is pleasant to live and spend our days: such are the good-tempered, and those who are not too ready to show us our mistakes, and those who are not cantankerous or quarrelsome—such [negative] people are always wanting to fight us, and those who fight us we feel wish for the opposite of what we wish for ourselves—and those who have the tact to make and take a joke; here both parties have the same object in view, when they can stand being made fun of as well as do it prettily themselves."
- **SOMEONE WHO LIKES OUR OWN BEST QUALITIES:** "And we also feel friendly towards those who praise such good qualities as we possess, and especially if they praise the good qualities that we are not too sure we do possess." Show your hero honoring the things your readers honor, and they'll engage with your hero.

- **THE ONE WHO LIVES IN WAYS WE APPROVE OF:** "And [we feel friendly] towards those who are cleanly in their person, their dress, and all their way of life." In other words, know your audience and show the character behaving in ways that the audience will find praiseworthy. The reader is looking for someone who is like her, after all, so the more ways you can show that they are similar, the more easily the process of *transportation* will occur.
- **THE ONE WHO IS FRIENDLY AND QUICK TO FORGIVE:** "Those who do not nurse grudges or store up grievances, but are always ready to make friends again; for we take it that they will behave to us just as we find them behaving to every one else."
- **THE ONE WHO CHOOSES TO BELIEVE THE BEST ABOUT OTHERS:** "And [we feel friendly] towards those who are not evil speakers and who are aware of neither their neighbours' bad points nor our own, but of our good ones only, as a good man always will be."
- **THE ONE WHO WOULD BE OUR ALLY:** "And [we feel friendly] towards those who do not try to thwart us when we are angry or in earnest, which would mean being ready to fight us." Remember that when transportation has happened, the reader almost comes to believe that the protagonist is him or her, so a character who is the hero's ally feels like the reader's ally.
- **THE ONE WHO LIKES US:** "And [we feel friendly] towards those who have some serious feeling towards us, such as admiration for us, or belief in our goodness, or pleasure in our company; especially if they feel like this about qualities in us for which we especially wish to be admired, esteemed, or liked." Again, a character who likes the hero is someone we like, because we identify with the hero.
- **THE ONE WHO IS LIKE US:** "And [we feel friendly] towards those who are like ourselves in character and occupation. … And those who desire the same things as we desire."

- **THE LOYAL FRIEND:** "And [we feel friendly toward] those who feel as friendly to us when we are not with them as when we are—which is why all men feel friendly towards those who are faithful to their dead friends. And, speaking generally, towards those who are really fond of their friends and do not desert them in trouble; of all good men, we feel most friendly to those who show their goodness as friends." Any time someone like Aristotle feels that some element of storytelling is so universally true that "all men feel" a certain way about it, the storyteller should take note.
- **THE HONEST AND FAITHFUL COUNSELOR:** "Also [we feel friendly] towards those who are honest with us, including those who will tell us of their own weak points." Likewise, the character who is an honest and faithful counselor to the hero is someone we like, as we feel connected to the hero.
- **THE ONE WHO MAKES US FEEL SAFE:** "We also like those with whom we do not feel frightened or uncomfortable—nobody can like a man of whom he feels frightened." And any time Aristotle says there is a storytelling principle that nobody can like, the storyteller should likewise pay attention.

If you want to know how to show that your character is a friend, Aristotle spells it out for you: "Things that cause friendship are: doing kindnesses; doing them unasked; and not proclaiming the fact when they are done, which shows that they were done for our own sake and not for some other reason."

There you have it: a voice from across the millennia instructing you in how to connect your reader to your hero.

KINDNESS

Another way to connect your reader to your hero is to show your hero being kind.

First, Aristotle's definition of kindness: "Helpfulness towards some one in need, not in return for anything, nor for the advantage of the helper himself, but for that of the person helped."

"Kindness is great," he says, "if shown to one who is in great need, or who needs what is important and hard to get, or who needs it at an important and difficult crisis; or if the helper is the only, the first, or the chief person to give the help."

Even a small help in a moment of need is a great kindness: "Those who stand by us in poverty or in banishment, even if they do not help us much, are yet [exceptionally] kind to us, because our need is great and the occasion pressing." The friend in need who offers even a cup of cool water to someone downtrodden is, as the famous vultures from Disney's *The Jungle Book* remind us, a friend indeed.

It follows that the refusal of such small help, or the giving of it but for some self-serving reason, is actually an act of exceptional unkindness. You can take most of these attributes and turn them into negatives when you want the reader to dislike someone.

How to show unkindness: "As evidence of the want of kindness, we may point out that a smaller service had been refused to the man in need; or that the same service, or an equal or greater one, has been given to his enemies; these facts show that the service in question was not done for the sake of the person helped. Or we may point out that the thing desired was worthless and that the helper knew it: no one will admit that he is in need of what is worthless."

Likewise, if you want more ways to show that your hero is kind, just have him do the opposite of these unkindnesses.

PITY

Aristotle's definition of pity is that it is the emotion you want your reader to feel when she sees good people suffering: "Pity may be defined as a feeling of pain caused by the sight of some evil, destructive or painful, which befalls one who does not deserve it, and which we might expect to befall ourselves or some friend of ours."

To make us feel pity—or compassion—toward your hero, you can show her or someone close to her experiencing one or more of the following: "Death in its various forms, bodily injuries and afflictions, old age, diseases, lack of food. … Friendlessness, [absence from] friends (it is a pitiful thing to be torn away from friends and companions), deformity, weakness, mutilation; evil coming from a source from which good ought to have come; and the frequent repetition of such misfortunes."

I suspect you could write a scene or more for each of those. If you want your reader to connect with your hero, and I'm pretty sure you do, show your hero going through some pain or tragedy or misfortune. Your reader will reach out in compassion—which is another way of saying that she will engage with your hero.

I think the following is fascinating in light of Dr. Zak's research about transportation, in which the hero is in trouble and *our* palms begin to sweat: We have compassion upon "those whom we know, if only they are not very closely related to us—in that case we feel about them as if we were in danger ourselves. For this reason Amasis did not weep, they say, at the sight of his son being led to death, but did weep when he saw his friend begging: the latter sight was pitiful, the former terrible."

Aristotle concluded that we'll have the most compassion on someone who is like us: "Also we pity those who are like us in age, character, disposition, social standing, or birth; for in all these cases it appears more likely that the same misfortune may befall us also. Here too we have to remember the general principle that what we fear for ourselves excites our pity when it happens to others." This is transportation language. If your reader is of a certain age or condition in life, it might behoove you to make your protagonist of similar age or condition.

Aristotle found that we will feel most compassionate when we see admirable or innocent people suffering: "Most piteous of all is when, in such times of trial, the victims are persons of noble character: whenever they are so, our pity is especially excited, because their innocence, as well as the setting of their misfortunes before our eyes, makes their misfortunes seem close to ourselves."

If you show how like your reader your hero is, and if you cause your hero to suffer, your reader will powerfully connect with your protagonist and your book.

INDIGNATION

The flipside of making your reader feel compassion toward your protagonist is making her feel indignant toward someone the protagonist encounters. Like the villain.

The more reader emotions you can arouse—so long as they're in service to your book and the reader is not mad *at* you, for instance—the more ways she will engage with your story.

A surefire way to make the reader feel indignant, Aristotle says, is to show bad people prospering. "It is our duty both to feel sympathy and pity for unmerited distress, and to feel indignation at unmerited prosperity; for whatever is undeserved is unjust."

Inequality bothers us, he says: "It is an injustice that those who are not our equals should have been held to deserve as much as we have. ... We loathe any kind of injustice."

Take someone we don't like and show him getting a raise or a prize, and we'll be upset, especially if it's something we feel the hero should've gotten. It's yet another tool to engage your reader's emotions in support of your protagonist.

EMULATION

Next, Aristotle turns to emulation (admiration). How can the writer cause the reader to feel connected to the hero? One way is to make the reader admire him and want to be like him.

"Emulation is [a sort of psychological] pain caused by seeing the presence, in persons whose nature is like our own, of good things that are highly valued and are possible for ourselves to acquire," Aristotle says. "But [admiration] is felt not because others have these goods, but because we have not got them ourselves. It is therefore a good feeling felt by good persons, whereas envy is a bad feeling felt by bad persons. Emulation makes us take steps to secure the good things in question."

If your reader is noble minded and you show a character behaving admirably, the reader will be inspired and encouraged to improve his own behavior. According to our dear philosopher, these are a few qualities that, if we see them in a character, we will admire and want for ourselves: "Wealth, abundance of friends, public office, courage, and the like." We also admire the things arising from our own heritage, he thinks: "We also feel [admiration] about anything for which our ancestors, relatives, personal friends, race, or country are specially honored, looking upon that thing as really our own, and therefore feeling that we deserve to have it."

Finally, Aristotle feels that we tend to admire the morally upright: "Further, since all good things that are highly honored are objects of emulation, moral goodness in its various forms must be such an object, and also all those good things that are useful and serviceable to others: for men honor those who are morally good, and also those who do them service."

Conversely, it follows that we will dislike someone for doing the opposite: "Those [readers] who are [predisposed] to emulate … are inevitably disposed to be contemptuous of all such persons as are subject to those bad things which are contrary to the good things that are the objects of emulation: despising them for just that reason." If a character spits on an American flag or does something else we consider vile behavior, we'll probably start hating that character.

SUMMARY

Who knew that a dusty old teacher carved in marble would have something to say about modern fiction, or that his comments would mesh so perfectly with cutting-edge brain science?

It was fun for me to see how much Aristotle's teachings in *Rhetoric* matched my own teachings about how to connect the reader to the protagonist. I've taught novelists to connect the reader to the protagonist by showing him being kind or generous or heroic or against tall odds, or even suffering disappointments and setbacks. It just goes to show that storytellers have been doing it right for a long time, even before we knew anything about neurotransmitters.

In these three chapters, we've heard from three wise men: Joseph Campbell, Carl Gustav Jung, and Aristotle. All of them discovered intensely effective means of communicating to hearers of story. Whether it is the sequence of the story itself, the characters populating it, or the ways readers are made to feel about them, these elements are all tremendous methods to make our fiction more likely to engage our readers' brains. If these storytelling tools have served yarn-spinners well over the generations, there's probably some powerful brain chemistry going on under the hood.

Pick and choose which aspects of this material you want to use, and do so knowing you're adding strand upon strand of connection between your reader and your story. Get enough of these things going in your favor, and you'll have a story that keeps your reader engaged from beginning to end.

CONCLUSION

The people who sit down to read your novel are like people filing into an auditorium to watch a magic show performed by a famous illusionist.

They know it's not real magic, but they don't care. *They want to believe.* They want to suspend their disbelief, and for ninety minutes they want to be amazed. They want to wonder how the magician did it—but not really. They'd rather call it magic, even if they know they're fooling themselves for fun.

In fact, they come into the auditorium *already* believing. If they hadn't wanted to see magic, they wouldn't have come to a magic show. They've come more than halfway toward the suspension of disbelief that's required. If the illusionist came out and bowed, the audience might think he'd done something magical that they won't see until later. And when the real show begins, they'll be clapping and *ooh*ing at full force.

The magician would have to be really bad to lose an audience like this. He'd have to make so many mistakes that the goodwill the audience had predeposited would become depleted and overdrawn. Then they'd get up and leave.

Two important things to notice here. First, the audience is eager to believe. They're throwing out all kinds of tendrils of connection and goodwill, already anticipating the fun they're going to have—probably because they've had fun at other magic shows in the past and they want to feel that way again. They're hoping to flirt again with almost believing, like they did as children, that magic might really exist.

Second, the audience doesn't care about the illusionist's craft. The audience doesn't even want the craft to be visible. They don't (usually) want the magician to stop his show and explain how every trick was done. If the showman's craft becomes the focus, the magic dissipates in, well, a cloud of smoke. Remember that: The audience doesn't want to know or even notice the magician's technique. How it happens is immaterial to fans of magic. What the audience wants is the magic itself.

So it is with readers of fiction. They don't want to know that you consciously avoided using buried dialogue. You can bury or dig up as much dialogue as you want—so long as the magic reigns supreme. Nor do they want to know about your *-ly* adverbs or your avoidance of a prologue or your use of gerunds or dialogue tags or characters with similar names.

All they want is the magic. All they want is to be swept away to a faraway land where a person who reminds readers of themselves is up against a terrible struggle and may not get what she's yearning for. All they want is to become someone else for awhile and have an adventure and perhaps a romance and maybe learn new ways to navigate some of life's narrow straits.

You, as a fellow magician-priest-storyteller, must learn the secrets of giving your readers the wonderment they're seeking. So we talk about oxytocin and adrenaline, transportation and struggle, hero's journeys, epic character types, and ways to elicit emotion. And we untangle ourselves from the spider's web of conflicting rules that would turn us into paralyzed husks of storytellers.

But the chief lesson we learn is not how to show our technique but how to hide it, so that our readers will find that it's ninety minutes later, or way past midnight, or that they've consumed the whole book in one sitting—and have no idea how it happened. The technique doesn't even matter, so long as the magic beguiles readers. Like a magician, we want to enchant our readers, to cast a spell on them that makes time disappear and allow the existence of only what we show them, our characters and our story. Stop worrying so much about the rules of fiction and start focusing on mesmerizing your audience.

Engage your reader from beginning to end, enthrall her as she wants to be enthralled, and you will have prevailed.

ABOUT THE AUTHOR

Jeff Gerke loves to empower novelists to tell the stories burning holes in their hearts. He does so through his how-to books for Writer's Digest, through the many writers conferences he teaches at every year, and through his own freelance mentoring and editing services at jeffgerke.com. He is the founder and former owner of Marcher Lord Press, a small science fiction and fantasy publishing company, and he is the author of multiple novels, including the Operation: Firebrand trilogy of military thrillers.

INDEX

action
  beginning with, 59–64
  falling, 160, 163
  rising, 160, 163, 168–173
adverbs, 114
  -ly adverbs, 31–35, 48–49, 72–75, 105
antagonists. See villains
anticipation, 170
archetypes, 139, 149, 181, 202–203
  the caregiver, 205–206
  the creator, 209–210
  the explorer, 206–207
  the hero (the warrior), 205
  the innocent, 203–204
  the jester, 210–211
  the lover, 208–209
  the magician, 212–213
  the orphan or everyman/everywoman, 204
  the rebel, 207–208
  the ruler, 213–214
  the sage, 211–212
  other archetypes, 214–215
  theory of, 131
Aristotle, 181, 216–226, 227
Austen, Jane, 66
backstory, 21, 147
  in first chapter, 127–128
beats, 74–75, 138
Bennington, Chester, 5
beta readers, 140
body parts, floating, 91–94
Bonds, Mitchell, 22–23
Bradbury, Ray, 61
brain chemistry, 148–150, 153, 163, 175–176
briefing scenes, 55
Campbell, Joseph, 131, 159, 181, 185, 191, 193, 201, 227
Character Therapist blog (Jeannie Campbell), 202
characters
  autobiographical protagonist, 135–136
  descriptions of, 117
  evil villains, 136
  introduction of, 89, 121, 123, 131
  likeable, 136
  mentor, 131
  multiple ways of referring to, 127
  names of, 121, 129
  point of view of, 142
  reader identification with, 179
  serving plot, 133
  stock, 214–215
  strong female protagonists, 130
  struggles of, 159–160
  teenagers as, 139
  thoughts of, 122
  traditional, 139
  vulnerability of, 158
  See also archetypes; protagonists; stereotypes; villains
Chiles, Robin, 183
Clancy, Tom, 68
Clarke, Arthur C., 212
cliché words and phrases, 115–116, 122
climax, 160, 163, 173–175
comic relief, 173
Crichton, Michael, 133–134
Crimson Petal and the White, The (Faber), 26
critique groups, 13, 124
Da Vinci Code, The (Brown), 170
Day, Vox, 22
denouement, 160, 163, 173–175
descriptions, 25–30, 122–123
  of characters, 117
  descriptors vs. disambiguators, 122–123
deux ex machina, 133, 198
dialogue, 32, 72–77, 124
  beginning a scene with, 128–129
  buried, 125
  complete sentences in, 140
  dialect, 32, 116–117
  ellipses in, 137
  grammar in, 97
  length of, 141–142
  in opening pages, 136
  speech attributions, 72–77
  unattributed, 129
  unimportant, 130
dialogue tags, 138
Dickens, Charles, 66
disambiguators, 122–123
dramatic arc, 160
dream sequences, 126
Durst-Benning, Petra, 61
editing, 134
emotional connection, 154–155. *See also* reader engagement

exposition. *See* opening scenes
Eye of the World, The (Jordan), 52
Faber, Michel, 26
Fahrenheit 451 (Bradbury), 61
Faulkner, William, 109
Ferris, Joshua, 66
fiction
  agenda-driven, 124–125
  for teens, 121
Finding Your Visual Voice: A Painter's Guide to Developing an Artistic Style (Mitchell & Haroun), 16
first-person point of view (POV), 65–70, 139
flashbacks, 125–126
floating body parts, 91–94
45 Master Characters (Schmidt), 202
fourth wall, 100–103
Franzen, Jonathan, 66
Freytag, Gustav, 160, 163
Fry, David F., 36–37
Garrett, James Leo, 17
gender lines, writing across, 143
generic narrator voice, 124
genre conventions, 120
gerunds, 95, 97–98
grammar rules, 95–99
Haroun, Lee, 16
hero. *See* hero's journey; protagonists
Hero with a Thousand Faces, A (Campbell), 182, 185
Hero, Second Class (Bonds), 22
hero's journey, 131, 139, 149, 159, 160, 181–183, 201
  apostasies, 195
  atonement with the father, 193–194
  the belly of the whale, 188–189
  the call to adventure, 185
  crossing the first threshold, 187–188
  crossing the return threshold, 198–199
  freedom to live, 200
  magic flight, 197–198
  master of two worlds, 199–200
  meeting with the goddess, 190–192
  the refusal of the call, 186
  the refusal of the return, 196–197
  the road of trials, 189–190
  the shape of the journey, 183–185
  supernatural aid, 187
  the ultimate boon, 195–196
  woman as the temptress, 192
Housekeeping (Robinson), 38
hyperbole, 92
inciting incident, 41–46
information dumps, 21, 55
internal monologue, 32, 124
Irving, John, 66
italicization, of characters' thoughts, 122
Jordan, Robert, 52, 57
Jung, Carl Gustav, 131, 181, 202, 227
King, Stephen, 109
length
  of novel, 120–121
  of opening scenes, 121
  of paragraphs, 123
Leonard, Elmore, 113–118, 145
literary fiction, 39
loose ends, 130
Lord of the Rings trilogy (Tolkien), 23, 75, 121, 185–190, 195, 198–199, 203–204, 213
Lost World, The (Crichton), 133–134
Lucas, George, 23, 201. See also *Star Wars* series
Ludlum, Robert, 170
McKee, Robert, 144
Miller, Henry, 167
mirror trick, 131–32
Mitchell, Dakota, 16
monologue, internal, 32, 124
monomyth. *See* hero's journey
Moral Molecule, The (Zak), 148
Morrissey, Tom, 145
Nietz, Kerry, 100
omniscient point of view (POV), 65–66, 68–69
opening scenes, 160, 163, 165–168
  action in, 59–64
  first lines, 59–60
  length of, 121
  themes in, 137–138
  See also prologues
Operation Firebrand-Origin (Gerke), 53–54
outlining, 78–82
pantsers, vs. plotters, 78–81
paragraphs
  beginning with character name, 141
  beginning with *I*, 142
  length of, 123
  order of, 140
  painted, 36–40
parentheses, 126
participial phrases, 96, 98
Plot Versus Character (Gerke), 81, 174
plot, outlining, 78–82
point of view (POV), 8–9, 65–71
  deep, 124, 141
  multiple, 68–69, 87
  number of characters, 142
prepositions, at the end of sentences, 96, 98
prologues, 20–24, 45, 89, 114. *See also* opening scenes
protagonists

autobiographical, 135–136
female, 130
inner journey of, 174
introduction of, 131
likeable, 136
name of, 140
need to fail, 143
sympathetic traits of, 157
worst things to happen to, 137
See also hero's journey
punctuation
ellipses, 137
exclamation points, 114–115
semicolons, 126
See also parentheses
purple prose, 36–40
questions
not in dialogue (QNID), 143–144
rhetorical, 127
so what? and *or else ... ?*, 129–130
reader engagement, 147–149, 178–179, 228–229
brain chemistry story map, 162–176
through characters, 156–161
through transportation, 150–155
readers
male vs. female, 160
opinions of, 7–9
parts skipped by, 117
writers as, 18–19, 109–112
reading, 109–112
rest points, 171–172
Rhetoric (Aristotle), 181, 216
emulation, 225–226
friendliness, 219–222
indignation, 225
kindness, 222–223
pity, 223–225
three means of persuasion, 217–218
use of emotions, 218–219
Robinson, Marilynne, 38
Russo, Richard, 20
Schmidt, Victoria Lynn, 202
second-person point of view (POV), 65–66, 69
sentences
beginning with *and*, 96
complete, 140
ending with prepositions, 96, 98
fragments, 96
varying structure and length, 131
setting, real vs. fictitious towns, 129
Shakespeare, William, 172
showing vs. telling, 51–58, 147
stage direction, 139
Star Wars series (Lucas), 22–23, 44, 185–192, 194–195, 197, 201, 205, 208, 211
Stengl, Anne Elisabeth, 66
stereotypes, 135, 202, 214–215
Story (McKee), 144
storylines, 87–90
summarizing, 55
Systematic Theology (Garrett), 17
telling, vs. showing, 147
themes, 124–125
in opening pages, 137–138
Then We Came to the End (Ferris), 66
theory of mind, 151, 153
third-person point of view (POV), 65–70
three-act structure, 132–133, 160
Tolkien, J.R.R., 121, 198. See also *Lord of the Rings* trilogy
Tolstoy, Leo, 66
transportation, 151–153, 155, 158, 221, 224
through plot, 159–160
Tropic of Cancer (Miller), 167
Twain, Mark, 116
Updike, John, 66
verbs
improper tenses, 99
passive voice, 96
said, 114
split infinitives, 137
subject-verb agreement, 99
"to be," 47–50
villains, 136, 183
Vogler, Christopher, 185
weather, avoiding, 113–114
Whitman, Walt, 39–40
Wolfe, Tom, 66
word choice, 104–108, 137, 142
all hell broke loose, 115–116
And, beginning a sentence, 96
could, 140
just, 141
look/looked, 142
only, 141
present tense, 120
suddenly, 115–116
that, 83–86
then, 115
weasel words, 104–108
See also adverbs; cliché words and phrases; verbs
word-order strangeness, 116
Worsnop, Danny, 5
Writer's Journey, The (Vogler), 185
writing what you know, 134
Zak, Paul J., 148, 150–153, 155–160, 162–172, 174–175, 178–179, 224